New Commonwealth Writing

A Critical Response

In the same series

Recent Commonwealth Literature (2 vols.)
R.K. Dhawan, P.V. Dhamija and A.K. Srivastava, ed.

Studies in Commonwealth Literature
K. Venkata Reddy

Commentaries on Commonwealth Poetry and Drama
S. Ramaswamy

Commentaries on Commonwealth Fiction
S. Ramaswamy

Commonwealth Writing: A Study in Expatriate Experience
R.K. Dhawan and L.S.R. Krishna Sastry, ed.

Centering the Margins: Perspectives on New Literatures in English from India, Africa and Australia
Cynthia vanden Driesen

New Commonwealth Writing

A Critical Response

M.L. Pandit

PRESTIGE

Published by
Prestige Books
3/28, East Patel Nagar
New Delhi 110 008

ISBN: 81-7551-007-2

1996

Reprinted 2000

Photo Typesetting by
Pivot Computers
Delhi 110 006

Printed at
Mehra Offset Press
New Delhi 110 002

Contents

AFRICA

CANADA

NOTES

Dedicated to

Professor S.L. Pandit
my father and teacher

Preface

This book is a collection of critical essays and notes written over a period spread across thirty-five years, 1961 to 1995. However, these are not placed in the chronological order in which originally written, but are arranged here according to their thematic connections to add to their coherence and unified meaning. For instance, while the very first essay is of a comparatively recent origin, the second was written thirty-five years ago in the centenary year of Rabindranath Tagore. Most of the essays are attempts at independent examination of the chosen authors, namely Tagore, Narayan, Rushdie, Bharati Mukherjee, Soyinka, Amadi, Margaret Laurence, Margaret Atwood, Rohinton Mistry, Vassanji and their novels. Yet some studies of a comparative character are also included in the collection. The first essay is a kind of general survey, and one of the notes evaluates a recent book of poems by a notable Indian writer. There is variety in the selection of the writers and their works, as also in the manner and treatment of the critical studies. Attention is paid to both thematic and technical aspects of the novels of the various authors.

Though all the essays and notes grouped here come under the broad category of Commonwealth literature, these do form sub-groups of those dealing with Indian, African and Canadian writers, respectively. In compilation, the critical essays are grouped first, followed by the notes. An interesting feature of the book is a hitherto unpublished interview with Salman Rushdie, which appears before the two essays on his prize-winning novel, *Midnight's Children*. This collection of essays should be of special interest to students and scholars involved in the study of different aspects of Commonwealth literature.

Acknowledgements

Grateful acknowledgement is made to the following for permission to reprint previously published material:

The editors of *English Studies in India*, Department of English, University of Kashmir, Srinagar, for "A Note on Sophocles' Oedipus and Narayan's Raju" and "West African Tribal Society in the Novels of Elechi Amadi."

Devindra Kohli, editor, *Indian Literary Review*, for "Native and Alien Grounds."

Ravi Nandan Sinha, editor, *The Indian Novel in English: Essays in Criticism*, for "Fantasy in Salman Rushdie's *Midnight's Children.*"

Some Expatriate Indian Writers in English: An Introduction

There was a time when English was the language of a vast British empire, over which the sun never set. That empire was wound up in the years following the second world war. But the English language still remains in the now independent countries, which once formed parts of the empire, as a convenient means of international communication. In all commonwealth countries, literary and critical works continue to be written in it. Although these nations have literary traditions in their own native tongues, yet English is employed in creative work deliberately and with zest. In contemporary times, people all over the world try to learn the use of English in some form or another. Wherever it is not the first language, it is still the second or third language. Whatever scientific research is carried out in any country, its conclusions are immediately available in English. Even in India, we have a special association with English. The British rulers went away from our country more than four decades ago, and yet we have not been able to give up their language. One can confidently say that the kind of writing in English that is being done now, and the standard that it has attained, were not there in India before independence.

The question, how far can English express the thoughts of the Indian writers, has a special importance. There is a point of view today that the Indian writers should not write in English, as it amounts to an almost anti-national act. Others are of the view that the Indian sensibility can develop and find proper expression only in an Indian language. When national writers write only for foreign audience, there is an apprehension that they cannot present the real picture of India. But every author has the freedom to choose the language in which he would prefer to write. Joseph Conrad was of Polish origin, yet he consigned his remarkable fictional creations to English. Samuel Beckett was Irish, still he preferred to live in Paris and write in French. The English language has grown deep roots in the Indian soil, and it is the language of the intelligentsia of this country. It is the language of our laws, courts and universities, and quite a few Indian writers have made a conscious choice in favour of English as their medium.

It is a pleasing thought to recall that not only in India, but abroad also—in countries like the USA, England and Canada—there are some authors of Indian origin who write in English. Their writings are judged to be of proven merit in these countries and in other parts of the world, wherever English is read and understood. Among these, the noteworthy are novelists like Raja Rao, Kamala Markandaya, Santha Rama Rau, Balachandra Rajan, and Bharati Mukherjee; masters of prose like Nirad Chaudhuri, Ved Mehta, Aubrey Menen, and Sasthi Brata, and a distinguished poet like Dom Moraes. All these are basically of Indian origin, and apart from Aubrey Menen and Dom Moraes, their mother tongue is one or another of Indian languages. Still, all of them, deliberately and by choice, write in English, and have a marked expertise in handling it.

Raja Rao is a notable writer of fiction, whose novel *Kanthapura*, published in London in 1938, had the distinction of being accepted early as a contribution to English literature. A Brahmin of the erstwhile princely state of Mysore, he was educated at Hyderabad, Montpellier and Paris. Marrying abroad, he lived for many years in France. Now, in his eighties, he divides his years between New York and India. E.M. Forster, the author of *A Passage to India*, declares that *Kanthapura* is a classic novel written in English by an Indian. It is the story of a small village in the former Mysore state in the twenties of the present century. With the backdrop of a vital turn in the history of the country, it could be the story of any Indian village caught up in the Satyagraha Movement launched by Mahatma Gandhi against the oppressive British rule. The novel very sensitively presents an authentic picture of how the movement reached this remote village and the painful repercussions it had on the life of the villagers. A shadow of Gandhi is found in Moorthy, who leads the Kanthapurians in this struggle. While writing a realistic epic novel of the freedom movement, Raja Rao also explores in his characteristic way the real nature of India.

The second novel of Raja Rao, *The Serpent and the Rope*, came out twenty-two years later, in 1960. This complex book makes an attempt to explore and explain his metaphysical vision of Indian culture, philosophy, religion and history. Encompassing little action, it is packed with monologues, dialogues, journals and descriptions. The book consists of the memoirs of Ramaswamy, a South Indian student, who, introspectively, narrates his marriage to Madeleine, an intellectual French girl. After the death of their children and the collapse of their marriage, he returns to India to seek his salvation by the traditional Indian methods. *The Serpent and the Rope* is a spiritual odyssey in which Ramaswamy comes back to the country of his birth after long years of exile in Europe. The novel could easily have become over-intellectualized, but the author succeeds in dramatizing the conflicts of the characters. However, it is a sophisticated work, employing many technical devices of the modern novel developed by James, Proust and Joyce. *The Cat and Shakespeare* (1965) is a short novel in which Raja Rao symbolically explores the Indian consciousness. It was followed by two other novels published at long intervals—*Comrade Kirillov* (1976) and *The Chessmaster and His Moves* (1988). In addition to these five novels, Raja Rao also produced a collection of short stories entitled *The Cow of the Barricades and Other Stories* (1947).

Among the contemporary popular Indian novelists in English, Kamala Markandaya enjoys a notable position. After studying at the University of Madras, she worked for some time as a journalist. Marrying an Englishman, she later settled in London, and started writing fiction. All her novels have been published in England. Living abroad, she continues to write on Indian themes. Out of a dozen works, the following five are more popular with her readers. The first novel, *Nectar in a Sieve* (1954), analyzes the life and inter-relationships of a peasant community. Markandaya pays special attention to the exploitation of her women characters by their men. *Some Inner Fury* (1955) is the story of an educated Indian girl and her English lover, who are separated and estranged after the 'Quit India' movement. *A Silence of Desire* (1960) deals with the life and concerns of an Indian middle-class family, while *A Handful of Rice* (1966) has urban poverty as its central theme. *The Coffer Dams* (1966) is about an English construction company and its project of building a multi-purpose dam on an Indian river. It is difficult to say how close an experience Markandaya has of all these diverse aspects of life in India, yet her characterization and skill in plot-structure are quite effective and successful. This is the reason behind her continued popularity with readers, both within and outside India.

Balachandra Rajan is a well-known literary critic, educationist and novelist. He made a name for himself in the academic circles at Cambridge University. At one time he was a member of the Indian Foreign Service. But he gave it up to become a university teacher, and for some years acted as the Professor and Head of the English Department at the University of Delhi. Now this colourful South Indian personality graces the academic life of Canada. His novel, *The Dark Dancer* (1959), reflects all those values that grace the sensibility and consciousness of a sensitive critic. It presents a realistic picture of the Indian turmoil in the post-independence years and the tragedies of the communal riots. Krishnan, educated in the West, returns to India to experience the usual tug-of-war of the cultures. Rajan's speciality is intellectualism and satirical characterization. Just as Raja Rao and Kamala Markandaya present a blend of the East and the West, the same trend is discernible in Balachandra Rajan also. Too Long in the West (1961) is another version of the East-West problem, but its treatment here is comic and satirical. Rajan succeeds in exploring with detached irony the dilemma of Nalini, when she returns to India after spending three years at Columbia University, the USA. The novel is all about the crisis of her confrontation with an India from which she feels alienated.

Santha Rama Rau is yet another Indian writer in English who followed Raja Rao, Markandaya and Rajan to the West, and lived there for long years. She wrote a dramatic version of Forster's *A Passage to India*, which was quite popular with the Western audiences. Then there is her novel *Remember the House* (1956) in which the heroine, Baba, spurns the Western culture, and returns to the tradition-bound India, where she finally finds peace. Though Rau's preoccupations are the private lives of her characters she concentrates on the tragic and heroic period of the Indian independence as a setting for her writing.

Bharati Mukherjee, a Calcutta-born Indian girl, went to the USA to attend a two-year creative writing workshop. There she met and married a Canadian writer named Clark Blaise. Thus was Bharati Mukherjee caught in the conflict of two cultures of the East and the West, which is the main concern of her writings. After living for some years in Canada, Bharati Mukherjee and her husband moved to New York, where they are settled now. Apart from some collections of short stories, Bharati Mukherjee wrote two novels, *The Tiger's Daughter* (1971) and *Wife* (1975). Both these works concentrate on the cultural conflict of the East and the West, and each has a heroine of Indian antecedents, who suffers a culture-shock by going to the USA. Both present an imaginative rendering of Bharati Mukherjee's personal experience of going West and the after-effects of the culture-shock felt by her. *Days and Nights in Calcutta*, she wrote in collaboration with her husband. Bharati Mukherjee's success in shorter fiction is *The Middleman and Other Stories* (1989), which fetched her the National Book Critics Circle Award for fiction in the USA.

Aubrey Menen was born and bred in England. For a period, he acted as the Director of an experimental theatre in London. Later, he worked for some time in the English drama section of the All India Radio, and, for a while, even flirted with the film industry. Now he lives in Rome, writing novels and miscellaneous works. He is a class by himself among the contemporary literary critics. His distinguishing quality lies in aiming at amusement rather than reform. Although he does not possess a mastery of the social comedy like the outstanding satirists, Aldous Huxley and Norman Douglas, yet he bears comparison with these two writers. Without apology, Menen makes the novel a medium of expressing his intellectualism, and, therefore, his characterization is sketchy and incomplete. Besides, he does not care for the traditional form of the novel. Still his works, such as, *The Prevalence of Witches* (1947), *The Stumbling Stone* (1949), *Rama Retold* (1954) and *The Fig Tree* (1959) have impressed men of distinct literary taste.

Ved Mehta is remarkable for being a blind writer with an international reputation. Born and educated in the undivided Punjab of the pre-independence era, he is settled in New York. Occasionally, he visits India, but always goes back to the USA. Like several other writers before him, bitter and sad experiences of life have turned him a humorist. The right use of irony and treating life as a comedy are the special features of his literary works. Writing since 1957, he has produced such well-known books as *Face to Face* (1960), *Walking the Indian Streets* (1961), *Delinquent Chacha* (1967), *John is Easy to Please* (1971), and *Daddyji* (1972). These have made him equally popular in the East and the West.

This brief survey of some of the expatriate Indian writers in English would be incomplete without mention of that unique Bengali historian and master of prose, Nirad C. Chaudhuri. His first work, *Autobiography of an Unknown Indian* (1951), is an account of his early years till he grows to maturity and witnesses the departure of the British from India. The special feature of this history of his times is its prose style, wit and charm. Chaudhuri writes powerfully and disturbingly about British India and the relationship between the rulers and the ruled. In the process, he explores his own personality divided between two opposite cultures. Another literary virtue of the *Autobiography* is the author's masterly portraits of persons like his mother and places like his village, which at the Partition became part of East Pakistan (now Bangladesh). Living in England, Chaudhuri is fascinated with the British and their culture, and he writes about it in *A Passage to England* (1959), which is his ironic reply to the ideas on the Indo-British race-relationships developed by Forster in his famous novel, *A Passage to India.* In his third book, *The Continent of Circe* (1965), Chaudhuri tries to explain the uncharacteristic behaviour of the British in India, a perversity which he traces to the migration of the Aryans from Central Asia to the Indo-Gangetic plains. He relates it to climatic and geographical conditions of the land, which, in his view, transformed all those invading races who conquered India and settled in this land. Nirad Chaudhuri writes with a degree of scepticism that makes him one of those rare Bengalis, who are not over-awed by the genius and reputation of a literary giant like

Rabindra Nath Tagore, whom he denounces as a fake.

The last but not least of the writers under review is Dom Moraes, without whose mention this essay would be incomplete. This son of a celebrated Indian journalist, Frank Moraes, was educated at Jesus College, Oxford University. Instead of pursuing a conventional profession, Dom Moraes preferred to write poetry. His achievement as a poet in English was so outstanding that he bagged the prestigious Hawthorndon Award in 1958. After living and writing for many years in England, he became the editor of the Hong Kong based journal, *The Asian Magazine*. Among the Indian poets writing in English, he is perhaps the most distinguished. His themes, landscapes, metaphors and similes do not reflect Indianness but a cosmopolitan colour. In a pleasant but weighty style he communicates his personal and realistic experiences of life. If someone has a private problem, Dom Moraes does not provide him with the solution, but persists in trying to find solutions to his own problems. He recognizes love and life as the vital issues of life, and admits the necessity of persistent suppression of the Devil within us. Living in England, he raised his voice against racism in that country. *A Beginning* (1957), *15 Poems for William Shakespeare* (1964), *John Nobody* (1965), *Poems* (1955-65) are some collections of his poetry. He has also written *My Son's Father: An Autobiography* (1969) and some other miscellaneous writings in prose, all of which bear the imprint of his class. These days Dom Moraes divides his time between poetry and freelance journalism.

Three Novels of Rabindra Nath Tagore

Rabindra Nath Tagore, the only Nobel Laureate in Literature that the sub-continent has produced so far, needs no introduction to Indian readers. His is a versatile genius that overwhelms all who come under the sway of his writings. If his brilliance is more prominent as a poet, dramatist, philosopher and educationist, he shines equally well on the Indian scene as an artist, essayist, story-teller and novelist.

During Tagore's boyhood, Bankimchandra Chattopadhyaya was producing powerful Bengali novels suffused with romantic patriotism, in quick succession. *Durgesh Nandini*, published in 1860, was a sort of forerunner in the field of Indian fiction. It decided the line that Indian novelists were to take. Bankimchandra followed it up with several historical, social and philosophical novels. The immediate success and popularity of these novels was immense.

And it was in this atmosphere of Hindu nationalism that Rabindra Nath Tagore grew up to youth and manhood. Starting his literary career as a poet, he gained complete mastery over his art with startling rapidity. Even before his thirtieth year, he was regularly writing lyrics, plays, essays, short-stories and novels of great charm. The influence of Bankimchandra may be easily traced in Tagore's early prose and novels. But this influence is not all-pervading and excessively pronounced. It is of a restrained nature. Instead of rigidly following the tradition of Bankimchandra, Tagore turned the Bengali novel into new channels. He was more interested in psychological delineation and the spiritual growth of his characters than in mere romantic patriotism. From 1901 to 1907, he wrote most of his novels in between his more celebrated poetical and dramatic works. But only three of these could be considered as worthy of note. These are *Eyesore, The Wreck* and *Gora*.

Eyesore, the first of Rabindra Nath Tagore's three great novels, was published in 1902. The title is a literal translation of the original Bengali "Chokher Bali," which is the playful name by which the two leading women characters of the novel call each other. This novel has been regarded as the first piece of modern fiction not only in Bengali but the whole of modern Indian literature. Tagore's earlier novels more or less conform to the Bankimchandra tradition. But here is something new—a study of the psychology of a young Hindu window. The plot centres round "the problem of human relationship" in a middle-class Bengali family of Calcutta. The main characters are only half a dozen in number. There is Rajlakshmi, a widowed mother, who dotes on her only son, Mahendra. Annapurna, the widowed sister of her dead husband, also lives with her. She is the affectionate 'Kakima' (auntie) of Mahendra and his bosom friend, Bihari, both of whom are studying medicine in a local medical college. Mahendra, the pampered and spoilt boy of his elders, is used to having his own way in all matters. Bihari is just the opposite of his friend. Having no parents of his own, he looks upon Mahendra's mother and aunt as his mother and aunt. He is far more considerate of other people's feelings than his more fortunate friend.

Of the other two characters, Asha is the innocent, affectionate, devoted but illiterate, wife of Mahendra. Her friend and a distant relation of the family is Binodini, the educated, cultured and charming young widow, who is the central figure in the novel. She should have been married to Mahendra, but for his obstinate refusal, when the match was suggested to him. Consequently, after being married to an ailing, middle-aged husband, she becomes a widow soon after her marriage. She is reduced to the state of "a lone garden-creeper in a jungle, a pathetic glory in joyless wilderness." But when Mahendra comes to know her rather intimately, he repents of his folly and turns to her at the cost of the happiness of his own home. "He was intoxicated by the prospect of a love, at once hidden and articulate, forbidden and forthcoming, poisonous and sweet, a love that was both a surrender and a challenge." Binodini's heart is full of a great sense of resentment against the society that unjustly deprives her of her right to love and happiness. A mocking, defiant fury against the whole world raged within her breast. "Like the enraged black-bee which stings whatever comes in its way, so Binodini, mad with rage, prepared to wreak her vengeance on the world around her, a world which seemed bent on thwarting her, spiting her." The woman in her clamours for what is denied her. She deliberately encourages Mahendra's infatuation for her. She chooses Mahendra as her victim for a special reason. She thinks that Mahendra, by rejecting her in the beginning, is partly responsible for her later plight. In this entanglement the persons who suffer most and come out of the fray as idealistic characters are Asha and Bihari. Asha is the last to know what is going on behind her back, and even then she needs the material proof of a letter to confirm her suspicions. At first suffering silently at her own failings, she finally finds consolation in the tranquillizing words of Kakima and her newly acquired regard in the eyes of her mother-in-law. Bihari suffers most of all. He loses not only his friend but also the regard of Asha and Kakima. The only thing that keeps him up is the service that he renders Rajlakshmi during the days of her illness, when even her son forsakes her. As the plot unfolds itself, Bihari secures greater admiration from other characters as well as from the reader. He ends up as a wandering saint. Asha and Mahendra are again united to each other, while Binodini realizes her mistake of running after the unattainable, and accepts Bihari as her *guru*.

The striking thing about the characterization of this novel is the way in which characters are presented in pairs. Asha and Binodini, Mahendra and Bihari, Rajlakshmi and Annapurna, act as perfect foils to each other. Each member of these pairs by his constant presence throws the other into relief, and thereby brings out the personality of the other as no accident, or dramatic situation could do. This method, which helps in revealing the psychology of the various characters, is something that we do not find in Bankimchandra. There is another aspect of the novel which shows that though Tagore is directing the Bengali novel into new channels, he is not completely free from the influence of his predecessor. The characters in the novel are constantly reading and discussing Bankimchandra's novels—*Visha Vriksh*, *Anand Math* and *Kapal Kundala*. The first mentioned has a special bearing on the plot of *Eyesore*, as that also deals with the unhappy life of a young widow. The chaste and figurative language of the novel is a special feature of Rabindra Nath Tagore's prose. The poet in him can never be curbed, as is evident from this passage: "As the dry, wilted stalks of the cornfield, when after a temporary drought the rains descend, suddenly turn green and shoot up vigorously, confidently, almost faintly as though eager to make up for the long bleak days of fast—so Asha blossomed into womanhood." On reading such passages one is reminded of the epic similes of Homer and Spenser.

After *Eyesore* comes *The Wreck*, which does not give evidence of any marked improvement in the technique of the writer. For its sheer realism, some writers regard the former novel superior to the latter. The initial incident, on which the plot of *The Wreck* hinges, is rather improbable, if not wholly impossible. But once the reader reconciles himself to the idea of a storm in the Hooghly, which throws one man's bride into the arms of another, all other events follow in an order which seems quite natural. Another aspect in which *The Wreck* may be considered inferior to *Eyesore* is that it does not deal with a general social problem, but with a highly improbable situation in the life of a youngman. The situation is ultimately resolved in as unconvincing a manner as it had started. The great thing is that it does resolve itself somehow or other. Considering the perplexity of Ramesh, whose life is in the end "wrecked" without any hopes of redemption, one almost comes to think that it will never be set right.

What sustains the interest of the reader through the four hundred pages of the novel is once again the realistic portrayal of characters. There are Ramesh, the conscientious young lawyer, and his friends, Jogendra and Akshay. Akshay acts the part of a well-meaning and semi-villain, who is up against Ramesh. Jogendra is a flat character, whose only job seems to be to act the part of the heroine's brother. Hemnalini is an educated and well-bred charming young Brahmo girl, who sincerely loves Ramesh. She trusts him in spite of an inexplicable change in his behaviour towards her. Kamala is the innocent and unsuspecting young bride who, though more experienced in household affairs, reminds one of the Asha of *Eyesore*. What Ramesh feels on seeing her for the first time is sufficient evidence of her sweetness: "As a painter enthrones in his heart the perfect picture, and then lavishes all his devotion on it, so Ramesh enshrined this slip of a girl in his fancy as his heart's delight and the bringer of joy and prosperity to his home." Her later tragedy is summed up in these words: "If only she had a little home somewhere! But where?" Her consolation in the days of her grief is Umesh, the orphan child, who looks at her as his mother, and follows her as a slave. The inevitable ideal characters in the novel are three. Trailokya Chakarbartti, better known as "Uncle Chakarbartti" of the whole West-Country, comes to Kamala's rescue in her distress. Dr. Nalinaksha is the surprising youngman who marries Kamala at the word of a friend, and then loses her for nearly a year. He is a brilliant speaker on problems of social reform, and is capable of carrying the whole audience with him as soon as he mounts the platform. His mother, Kshemankari, guards her Brahmin caste with utmost rigidity. Still she is broad-minded enough to suffer her Brahmo son, and is at one stage prepared to welcome a daughter-in-law of the same sect into her house. The charm of her personality comes out best in her relationship with Kamala, when she does not know her as the wife of her son. Hemnalini's kind-hearted and gentle father, Ananda Babu, could be another ideal character, but for his weakness not to upbraid Jogendra and Akshay openly. His eccentricities, arising from the constant attention that he pays to his suspected stomach ailment, provide some of the much needed humour in an otherwise serious novel.

Whatever criticism may be levelled against Rabindra Nath Tagore's novels, there can be no two opinions about it that *Gora* is a masterpiece. Here is what an English critic thinks of *Gora*: "Between 1901 and 1907 he [Tagore] wrote most of his novels. The first two, *Eyesore* and *The Wreck* are incredibly bad. A charming style and fine description are not enough in a novel; and the stories are botched. *Gora* came at the end of this period of novel writing. It is a book, which has greatly influenced Bengali novelists, and by some it is held to be the best of the Bengali novels."[1] It seems that Thompson is somewhat hasty in his denunciation of the first two novels, but his opinion about *Gora* is perfectly authentic and candid. In this novel it is not the intricacy of the plot and the rapid change-over from climax to anti-climax, as in *The Wreck*, but the clash of characters and their ideologies, and the final emergence and triumph of truth that holds the reader spell-bound.

Gora, Binoy, Paresh Babu, Sucharita, Lolita and Anandamoyi are not important for themselves alone, but for the ideals they uphold, the ideas they adhere to, and the truths they want to establish. The clash of the high-caste and the low-caste, the Brahmin and the Brahmo, is not the central theme of the novel. It is just for convenience's sake, for want of something better. It serves a secondary purpose, that of an accessory to the principal problem, which is of a spiritual as well as a philosophical nature. What is truth? How to realize it? What is the real problem facing British India? How is it possible to raise the Indians above their petty complexes? These are the questions that come to the minds of the main characters again and again. Gora thinks that his faith in the stability of Brahminism is the answer to all these questions. But he is disillusioned when he goes to the villages. He discovers that the strict regulations of his religion fail to unite the Hindus, whereas the Mohammedans were united by their religion. They stood shoulder to shoulder in a way that the Hindus never did. Perhaps it was due to their disregard of any caste-system. It is not easy to define what is Paresh Babu's idea of truth, in spite of his daily meditations according to the Brahmo ritual and the peace of mind that he derives from them, he himself does not seem to be quite sure about it. It is only by accident, while discussing with Sucharita the prospects of Binoy's marriage with his daughter, Lolita, that he hits at the truth: "Sectarianism is a thing which makes people entirely forget the simple and obvious truth that man is man—it creates a kind of whirlpool in which the society-made distinction between Hindu and Brahmo assumes greater importance than universal truth." Sucharita, with her unshakable faith in Paresh Babu, is drawn towards Gora. His beaming forehead and the force of conviction with which he speaks make her ponder over ideas which she has upto that time rejected as utterly unreasonable. Lolita believes in the inherent good qualities of Binoy, and tries to wean him from the destructive hold that Gora has over him. Binoy wavers between his adherence to Gora's views and the reverence that he feels for Paresh Babu. As he thinks that the sisterly affection of Sucharita and the love of Lolita is the truth, he gradually leaves Gora's circle and joins the group of Paresh Babu's admirers. Anandamoyi is an open-hearted and sincere old lady, who does not believe in the outward show of religion that her husband makes rather late in his life. She has absolute faith in her adopted son, Gora, who is the child of an Irish lady who came to their house one night in the troubled year of 1857, and died soon after giving birth to the child.

At first, it appears that Gora and Sucharita will never be united. But as soon as the mystery of Gora's birth is revealed to him, and he comes to know that he is not a Hindu, the effect is astonishing. "In a single moment Gora's whole life seemed to him like some extraordinary dream. The foundations upon which, from childhood, all his life had been raised had suddenly crumbled into dust, and he was unable to understand who he was or where he stood. . . . He felt as though he were like the dewdrop on the lotus leaf which comes into existence for a moment only. He had no mother, no father, no country, no nationality, no lineage, no God even." He at once rushed to Paresh Babu's house with the cry that he has no more ties: "That which day and night I have been longing for but which could not be, to-day at last I have become. To-day I am really an Indian! In me there is no longer any opposition between Hindu, Mussulman and Christian. To-day every caste in India is my caste, the food of all is my food! . . . Today I have become so pure that I can never be afraid of contamination even in the house of the lowest of castes. Paresh Babu, this morning with my heart absolutely bare, I have prostrated myself wholly at the knees of my India—after so long I have at length fully experienced what is meant by the mother's lap." What a moving conclusion to a great novel!

The rest of the characters are of minor importance. They are taken up with their own problems. Mohim, Gora's elder step-brother is keen to see his daughter married to a youngman who would not insist on a dowry. Krishandayal Babu is in search of some hidden short-cut to salvation. Baroda Sundari, Paresh Babu's wife, is on the lookout for eligible youngmen who would marry her daughters. Harimohini is intent on seeing her plans to marry her niece, Sucharita, to her own brother-in-law come true. Satish is just a child with a child's problems and interests. Of these characters, only Haran Chandra draws some special attention from the reader. That also, because he is the villain of the piece, and serves as a butt for Gora to sharpen his argumentative faculties.

These are three great novels of one of the most famous men of letters of the East. Rabindra Nath Tagore filled the whole of our literary horizon with his personality during his life-time, and continues to do so even after his passing away. In conclusion, I may add what one of his admirers thinks of him: "Judged by any standards whatsoever, Tagore's many-sided achievements must compel recognition, and he is not of Bengal alone, but India's and the world's."[2]

NOTES

1. Edward Thompson, *Rabindra Nath Tagore, Poet and Dramatist* (Oxford University Press), p. 194.
2. K.R.S. Iyengar, *The Indian Writing in English.*

A Woman Looks at the Changing Indian Muslim Society: Attia Hosain's *Sunlight on a Broken Column*

Inspired by the example of the nineteenth century novel in England, the twentieth century Indian novel in English is usually a document of social criticism. The feminine writers, reflecting the experiences of the Indian women, have a tendency to project their social consciousness in their novels. Whether it is Kamala Markandaya, Nayantara Sahgal or Anita Desai, all of them write about the trials and tribulations of the Indian woman, in whatever historical, social, cultural, and communal set up she is placed. It is always a struggle for her to lift herself above the quagmire of social and religious taboos in order to hold her own in a male-dominated society. Meena Shirwadkar rightly says, "The early fiction by Indian women in all Indian languages was an effort to give expression to their agonies and sufferings."[1]

Up to the middle of the century, the plight of the Muslim women in India was particularly sad, and, in some cases, it continues to be the same even now, due to the traditional purdah system and the resultant exploitation of women by their men-folk. This made it very difficult for a Muslim girl to get a modern education in the manner of the boys. But there are always exceptions to the given circumstances. Attia Hosain is one of those exceptions. Having lost both her parents early in life, she grew up in her grandfather's house as part of a feudal *taluqdar* family of the pre-independence United Provinces (later renamed as Uttar Pradesh). Somehow, she managed to get an English education at Lucknow, and, rather late in life, wrote her experiences from the age of fifteen to fifty in an autobiographical novel, *Sunlight on a Broken Column.*[2]

The *taluqdars* of the United Provinces had evolved a code of feudal honour, which, in contradiction to the medieval European code, was harsh towards the women. Confining the ladies to a secluded life behind the purdah, the men flaunted the code by patronizing the courtesans of Lucknow. Sowing the proverbial wild oats was considered part of the training schedule of a dashing aristocratic young man of culture and breeding. But this exclusive air of freedom was reserved only for the men, while the women languished at home, their fate dependent on the whims and vagaries of a father, uncle, husband, brother or son. Belonging to this society, Attia Hosain grew up between the two worlds of tradition and modernity. Living within the restrictions of the one, she hungered for the freedom of the other, and gradually moved towards it. About her girlhood, Mulk Raj Anand writes in "Attia Hosain: A Profile": "I imagined this young lady growing up as a golden bird, protected, enclosed and sustained as a parrot in a cage."

But Attia grew up with an open mind and a consciousness that she was justified in casting doubts on what did not appear right to rationality and reason. What she could not say in public, as there were no opportunities for her to do so, she communicates in a remarkable work of fiction, *Sunlight on a Broken Column*. It is the novel of her youth, in which she fictionally recreates her past, present and thoughts of the future. The past is not hers alone but of an entire decadent generation, as part of which she grows from childhood to adolescence, early youth of maturity, without too much of a sense of regret over the passing pageant of time.

Attia Hosain's book is one of the few deeply sensitive Indian novels in English of the sixties of the twentieth century. Laila, the heroine, is modelled on Attia herself, and through her eyes we look at the precariousness of life in India of the first half of the century. Laila's recollections expose the denseness of a decadent society that tries to hold on to the traditions at all cost. In Laila's narrative, the poor relations and servants are, significantly, more sympathetic and perceptive of the young girl's desire for social freedom, while the elders of her clan, of both sexes, try incessantly to shut her up in the 'cage.' Remembering the past has a special symbolic significance of its own, the 'Ashiana,' where Laila spends the formative years of her childhood, becomes the symbol of a home, to which she returns in the final sequence of events. It provides both a stimulus and backdrop to her memories of the happenings of nearly a decade and a half of the immediate past in her life. The panorama of the vividly remembered moments, presented in all their dramatic intensity, is deeply moving and poignant.

As *Sunlight on a Broken Column*—the title, incidentally, is borrowed from "The Hollow Men" of T.S. Eliot—unfolds, the orphaned Laila is an adolescent girl of fifteen. She lives with her two aunts, Majida and Abida, in the 'Ashiana' of her grandfather, Baba Jan, who is lying on his death-bed. Dependent on the mercies of the elders, Laila and her cousin, Zahra, feel their girlhood a heavy burden. Hakiman Bua, the old nurse, constantly asks Laila to pull her head out of her books and look at the surrounding world. But the broad outer world of the books fascinates her more than the narrow inner world of her society. The immediate question of paramount importance is what would happen after the death of Baba Jan. At fifteen, for Laila, the years are endless corridors of time stretching before and after. Aunt Abida understands her strange urges, and encourages them by sending her to an English convent school. But the dark clouds of the disciplines of a tradition-bound social order are ominously hovering over the horizon. When the matter of Zahra's marriage comes up for discussion in the family conclave, and Abida mentions the necessity of asking the girl's opinion on that issue, Uncle Mohsin is shocked and angrily shouts, "Is the girl to pass judgement on her elders? Doubt their capacity to choose? Question their decision? Choose her own husband?" (20)

The elder generation believes in the wisdom of their seniors, and that is a good enough system for them. But the youth question the time-worn norms. As the author bitterly comments, looking for suitable young men for the daughters of the family is like choosing a new horse for the carriage of the *taluqdar*. In the opinion of Uncle Mohsin, Zahra has read the Quran, she knows her religious duties, she can sew and cook, and at the *maktab* she has picked up a little English, which is what young men want in a bride. We are told that this very 'pious' uncle Mohsin would have liked to outrage the modesty of the servant girl, Nandi, had she let him do it. Such is the ironic diversity of the double social standards. Oppressed by her rebellious thoughts, Laila boldly declares to Zahra, 'I won't be paired off like an animal.' (29) Aware of the state of mind of her niece, Aunt Abida cautions Laila, "My child, there are certain rules of conduct that must be observed in this world without question. I do not wish anyone to point a finger at you, because it will be a sign of mine failure. Never forget the family into which you were born." (38) Laila wants to ask her why she was sent to school among those other girls, who were not torn apart by doubts, why she was not brought up like Zahra, who meekly accepts the man selected by the family to marry her. Asad, a poor relation and distant cousin of the two girls, loves Zahra, and writes Urdu poems in celebration of his love. When Zahra smiles at Asad, his pale lips twitch and his eyes shine like his poems. But, unlike Laila, Zahra cares more for a successful marriage in the traditional sense of material gains and comfort than marrying for love. "The elderly ladies of the *taluqdar's* household sunned their age-corroded cold bones, mouthed soundless prayers, turned the beads of their *tasbhis*, and stared at the movement in the courtyard from the distance of their years." (49) As for the young, the life within the household encloses and cushions the mind and heart against the outside world, and again moves back to its patterned smoothness. When the *mujra* girls come to sing on a festive occasion, the critical eyes of Laila notice: "The naked eyes of young men and old, in silk and brocaded and embroidered *achkans* and rakish caps, were more aware of the conscious womanhood of the singers than of their artistry." (65) All the time, her heart aches for Asad, whose genuine love for Zahra is changed into a sin by conventions. Night after night, Laila lies on the common bed with her back to Zahra, "struggling with [her] confused thoughts, pity for Asad, anger at Zahra, impatience with her mother, wonder at the meaning of love and truth and duty." (81)

On a visit to the ancestral house in the village, Laila comes to know that the brides of the household were kept in the rooms behind a terrace. There husbands crept up the stairs at night, and left as stealthily before anyone was awake. Bewildered by such unreasonable behaviour, Laila asks, "if it is such a shameful business being married and having children, why talk of nothing but marriage from the moment a girl is born?" (105) No wonder, she rebels and decides early in her life to go away from such an irrational world. At Zahra's wedding, she notices the elder women are more anxious about the girl's dowry than about the man she is marrying. Laila, who thinks on a different plane from these tradition-bound women, asks of herself, "Why was I allowed to become different?" (115) What is she to believe in? Why is she different from Zahra? What is wrong with her? And, most important of all, what is to become of her? Tortured by doubt and dismay, she lives in two worlds, an observer in an outside world and solitary in her own. A privileged Muslim girl, studying English literature at the University, she reflects: "Our world was bounded by our books, and the voices that spoke to us through them were of great men, profound thinkers and philosophers and poets. . . . Always I lived in two worlds, and I grew to resent the 'real' world." (128) A core of intolerance hardens inside her against the hollowness of the ideas of progress preached by her aunts and their companions. She rebels against this hypocrisy but finds no outlet.

Laila's life changes. She feels restricted by invisible barriers as effectively as the physically restricted lives of her aunts in the Zenana. "A window had opened here, a door there, a curtain had been drawn aside, but, outside lay a world narrowed by one's field of vision." (173)

The conflicting values of the world that she lives in with her aunts Abida and Majida make her so full of doubts and questions that she retreats more and more within herself. But soon a ray of sunshine dispels the smothering darkness surrounding her. At the annual gathering of the *taluqdars*, a handsome young man comes to her rescue when she feels lost in a motley crowd of strangers. His name is Ameer, and they meet again in the company of Laila's cousins. Inevitably, the two fall in love with each other, but the family does not agree to their marriage. What could be more ironic than the fact that one who is named Ameer is actually poor, and has to take up an ill-paid job to make his living. Still Laila and Ameer continue to meet in secret, and keep alive their dream of being united in life. Laila's emotional liberation in love is expressed by Attia Hosain in these words: "The moment when Ameer kissed me had no beginning: it was as pure and eternal as the snows we had been watching in deep communicative silence. . . . I knew a sense of such completeness and harmony that it seemed I was the earth, the sky, the light and the snow." (222)

Even uncle Hamid, whom Laila considers emancipated due to his English education and liberal outlook, forbids Laila to marry against the wishes of the family. But love for Ameer gives her courage and strengthens her resolve to defy all—the time-worn social taboos, shackling social norms, family ties and physical barriers. For her it is a deliberate and consciously made break from the past and its traditions. It is a long leap towards modernity and freedom. The sacrifice that she makes does not come easily. Her greatest regret is separation from Aunt Abida, who is the nearest to a mother she has known in the years of her conscious girlhood and after. Laila's friend from school days, Sita, gives her a lesson in worldly wisdom: "You are a child dreaming romantic dreams of love. What has love to do with marriage? It is like mixing oil and water. Love is anti-social, while matrimony preserves the world and its respectability." (296)

Laila does not listen to Sita, but goes ahead and marries Ameer without the blessings of the elders of her family. They were happy together for a few short years. Laila feels fulfilled when a daughter is born to her. An official assignment takes Ameer abroad during the world war, and he perishes there in an encounter. That marks the end of Laila's short-lived happiness. Visiting 'Ashiana,' which is no longer occupied by the family, after fourteen years, she reflects, "I had been guilty of admitting I loved, and love between man and woman was associated with sex, and sex was sin." (312)

Laila looks at 'Ashiana' as a living symbol of the past with its eroded traditions. In its decay she sees all the years of the family remembered from her childhood onwards. She recalls the slow years that once evolved a way of life and the swift years that brought it to an end. The breaking up of a social order and the emergence of another is symbolized by the contrast between the reflection of the eager girl of fifteen that the mature but ravaged woman of fifty perceives in the mirror: "She was so different from me, that girl, whose yesterdays and todays looked always towards her tomorrow, while my tomorrows were always yesterday." (319)

Attia Hosain's *Sunlight on a Broken Column* reminds one of an earlier Indian novel in English, Ahmed Ali's *Twilight in Delhi.* In the Introduction, Ahmed Ali writes: "my purpose was to depict a phase of our national life and the decay of a whole culture, a particular mode of thought and living, now dead and gone already right before our eyes."[3] This declaration by the talented writer, who went to live in Pakistan after 1947, makes obvious the similarity of themes of the two novels. The parallelism is further highlighted by Begam Nihal's comment in Ahmed Ali's novel about a particular girl, who she thinks would be a suitable bride for her son, Asgar. "She is a nice girl and will be a very good housewife. She sews so well, and she is a very good cook. She will make Asgar very happy." (40)

Exactly the same point of view regarding a girl of marriageable age is expressed by Uncle Mohsin while considering a suitable match for Zahra. However, the difference between the two novels is that whereas Attia Hosain's work is introspective and, hence, limited, Ahmed Ali's is more broad-based and offers a vaster picture of the tradition-bound Muslim society of Delhi. That this society was open to the influence of cross-currents from Indian cultures is made clear by Ahmed Ali when he tells us something about the eldest sister of Asgar, who had become a widow at the age of nineteen. Though "Islam permitted her to marry again, the social code, derived mostly from prevailing Hindu practice, did not favour a second marriage." (27)

Attia Hosain gives a woman's view of the singing girls of Lucknow. But Ahmed Ali provides a balanced picture in making a distinction between two kinds of prostitutes, the cultured ones and whores. The former were patronized by the rich and well-to-do. Young men were "sent to them to learn manners and the art of polite conversation: and the older people came to enjoy their dancing, music, and their company in general." (29)

Twilight in Delhi is also remarkable for the detailed account of the marriage of Asgar and Bilqeece. That makes it a valuable record of social history, for a day might come when the ceremonies depicted in the novel would be only a nostalgic memory. "Bilqueece was made to wear red clothes and was brought out before the bridegroom's female relations. . . . They 'sweetened' her mouth with crystallized sugar and gave her a purse containing one hundred and one rupees. All this and other ceremonies were accompanied with different songs, and for each occasion, sung by domnis." (114) Equally satisfying is the poignant description of *Vida*, when a bride leaves the parental house to go away with her groom. In an Indian home, where the woman is relegated to a subordinate place, love enters very rarely. Asgar would have liked to hear Bilqueece talk of love and happiness. But, as Ahmed Ali writes, "she was a simple Indian girl, and did not know the ways of love." (132) Later in the novel, he dwells on the cruelty of the heart of man, when Asgar decides to marry again within less than six months of the death of Bilqeece.

In spite of the commonality of themes, *Sunlight on a Broken Column* and *Twilight in Delhi* are more satisfying when read together. The two notable works of fiction, though written in contrasting styles, are yet complementary to each other in terms of the combined light thrown on a dwindling and changing society. There is more of tradition in the latter, while the currents of modernity are powerfully felt in the former. Taken together, these two novels provide a complete picture of the North Indian Muslim society that is fast disappearing due to the winds of change. In this context one would do well in turning to *The Young Wife and Other Stories* by Zaib-un-Nissa Hamid-allah, a feminist from Pakistan. As she writes in the preface to her book, she strives "to depict the change that is gradually coming about in the relationship between man and woman in the rural areas of Pakistan where emotions are still frequently in a primitive stage and where romantic love is seldom known."[4] In "The Young Wife," the very first story in the collection, the author projects her intolerance of a woman's meek acceptance of the dominance by her unreasonable husband. She writes: "Thirty years of marriage had not succeeded in making man and wife companions. The wife was still conscious only of the maleness of the man and years of submissiveness had made her meek and subservient to her husband's slightest whim." (8) Aliya, the young girl, on whom the story is centered, rebels against convention, but it is not possible for her to escape the common fate of a grown up girl in a Muslim household. "Soon she would be given in marriage to some coarse, domineering male who would crush all the spirit of freedom within her soul, even as her mother and sisters had been cowed and broken by their husbands." (12) Considering her liberal attitude to life, though herself part of a narrow society, Aliya might well be a character out of the novels of Ahmed Ali and Attia Hosain.

NOTES

1. "Indian English Women Novelists," *Perspectives on Indian Fiction in English*, ed. M.K. Naik (New Delhi: Abhinav, 1985), p. 200
2. (1961; New Delhi: Arnold Heinemann, 1979).
3. (Hogarth Press, 1940; Delhi: OUP, 1991), p. viii.
4. (Karachi: The Mirror Publications, 1958), p. 5.

Woman as Protagonist: Self in Margaret Laurence's *The Diviners* and Bharati Mukherjee's *The Tiger's Daughter*

In a man's world it is but natural that woman should hold the centre stage in art and literature. This trend is noticed in the creative works of all languages, from the ancient classical epics to the modern novel. Just consider these well-known figures in world literature: Helen, Clytemnestra and Medea of Greek literature; Sita, Draupadi and Shakuntala of Sanskrit literature; Cleopatra, Lady Macbeth and Vittoria of the English poetic drama; Madame Bovary and Anna Karenina of the European novel; Hester Prynne and Isabella of the American fiction; Emily Brontë's Catherine and Virginia Woolf's Mrs Dalloway. Obviously, the universal appeal of woman as a central figure in literature is equally true of the writings of men and women. If a special attraction of the Shakespearean drama is its galaxy of tragic heroes, the attention of the readers and critics is also drawn to Rosalynd, Desdemona, Ophelia and Cordelia. The women characters of George Eliot and the Brontë sisters are mentioned together with those of Dickens and Thackeray. In modern English fiction, both D.H. Lawrence and Virginia Woolf are singled out for their skilful delineation of women. But there is a difference of approach in the treatment of women between the writings of male and female authors. When feminine writers project women in fiction, they do adopt a special stance of their own. An attempt is made here to demonstrate that very individuality by examining a heroine each of Margaret Laurence and Bharati Mukherjee.

The element of the self in the female protagonists of feminine writers is a very important part of their psyche. In recording the development of their characters, the authors tend to reflect the pains of their own process of growing up, as writing for them is a way of self-realization. Margaret Laurence and Bharati Mukherjee both fall back upon their early experiences which they use as raw material for their literary works. This is established when one goes into the origins of the Manawaka series of Margaret Laurence, and the first two novels of

Bharati Mukherjee—*The Tiger's Daughter* and *Wife*.

Any similarity of origins does not, however, imply commonality of theme and approach in the two novelists. The nature of their experience and the use they make of it, each in her own place, are not of the same kind. As a young girl, Margaret Laurence went through a comparatively harsh childhood in the secluded society of a small Canadian prairie town, Neepawa in Manitoba. Only after leaving the town to go to college in the nearest city, Winnipeg, did she come to grips with the vaster and more varied outside world with its complexities of commerce and human relationships. The novelty and range of her new experience, away from her birthplace, enrich the quality and scope of *The Diviners*, the last of the Manawaka novels. It crowns Margaret Laurence's literary career with a work of fiction that remains the unchallenged masterpiece among her writings. One of the central themes of the novel is the struggle of Morag Gunn, the protagonist, for succeeding as a writer, and her sense of achievement on fulfilling her ambition. This echoes the ambition and success of the author herself.

Morag's desire to write does not receive much encouragement from her academic husband, Brooke Skelton. The Professor of English is wholly taken up with his own aspiration to rise in the university circles, and he does not bother about the intellectual needs of his wife. She finds him so incompatible a life partner that she decides on separation and manages to secure a divorce. It is while living alone and under severe economic stress that Morag's first novel is accepted for publication. The first book and her daughter come almost simultaneously, and thus her intellectual and physical fulfilments virtually coincide. After the initial success, Morag Gunn produces a succession of best-sellers. When she goes back to Manawaka to visit her foster-father, Christie Logan, on his sick-bed, the girl at the hospital reception desk feels proud of her.

> "I have read your books, Miss Gunn," the girl says shyly, "and I just want to say we're real glad you're from Manawaka. They've got your books in the library."[1]

It is a very touching moment in the life of Morag Gunn, a deeply felt experience that a successful Margaret Laurence herself must have or could have gone through on one of her visits to Neepawa. Like the author, Morag too goes across the Atlantic on a journey of discovery to locate her roots in Scotland, and, like the former again, she returns disillusioned, realizing that her real home is in colonial Canada, where she was born and bred up. This makes it more than evident that the projection of the self through the heroine is a leading concern of Margaret Laurence in *The Diviners*. Now, let us turn our attention to the other novelist under examination.

The early years of Bharati Mukherjee's sheltered life were spent as the dearly loved daughter of an upper class family of the metropolitan city of Calcutta. She had the advantage of a convent schooling, followed by higher education at a prestigious institute in the USA. She got her M.F.A. and Ph.D. from the University of Iowa, and worked for some years as Assistant Professor of English at McGill University, Montreal, before moving to New York along with Clark Blaise, her Canadian husband. Initially, like most Indian girls of her class and upbringing, Bharati Mukherjee must have looked at life through the proverbial coloured glasses, which were removed on her first hand contact with life in the West. Herself, she did not accept the caste system of her ancestors, but she encountered racial prejudice—a different kind of caste system—in Canada, when she went to live there. The culture shock experienced by Bharati Mukherjee was bound to change her as a woman and as a writer. What she went through at a personal level is reflected in the experiences of the heroines of her two novels, *The Tiger's Daughter* and *Wife*.

This is particularly true of the first work, in which the self of the writer is more intimately projected through the protagonist, Tara Banerjee Cartwright. The heroine of *The Tiger's Daughter* grows up, more or less, in the same environs as her creator. Though bred up in independent India, Bharati Mukherjee's mental set up, when she went abroad for higher education to the free and permissive society of the USA, still reflected the prejudices inherent to the educational system of a colonial convent school at Calcutta. This is a circumstance that is repeated in the experience of Tara. Her sense of culture shock on going abroad is a repetition of what the author herself experienced under similar circumstances. Like Bharati Mukherjee, she too returns to India and to her parents, as the young bride of a white man, whom they have yet to see and know. The novelist's sensitive presentation of the manner in which the friends and relations of Tara react to her changed status is a true reflection of what she herself went through in a Calcutta that is no longer the same as it was during her school days. Tara's nephews at Bombay call her 'the American Auntie,' and their parents refer to her husband as 'the American *Jamai*.' Aunt Jharna makes the difference clear by asking her pointedly, "You have come back to make fun of us, haven't you? What gives you the right? Your American money? Your *mleccha* husband?"[2] It makes Tara wonder: how does the foreignness of the spirit begin? And that is as much a problem of Bharati Mukherjee

Blaise as of Tara Banerjee Cartwright.

In *The Diviners*, Margaret Laurence projects the self through Morag Gunn, as a woman who seeks and achieves physical fulfilment by becoming the mother of a daughter, and also attains intellectual fulfilment by gaining recognition as a writer. Bharati Mukherjee projects the self in *The Tiger's Daughter* as someone who encounters a double culture shock—the first on going abroad to the USA for higher education, and the second on return to India as the bride of a Canadian writer. The priorities are different, the concerns are different, and the emphasis is different, because Margaret Laurence and Bharati Mukherjee—emancipated feminine novelists both—are, after all, two individual personalities with divergent social, cultural and geographical backgrounds, and, what is more important, they reflect two different experiences of life. It only shows the rich variety of the rhythms of life in a woman's world.

The two writers come from two diametrically opposite backgrounds. Margaret Laurence belongs to the permissive colonial society of the West that takes a tolerant view of the pre-marital and extra-marital affairs of Morag Gunn. When Brooke Skelton does not appreciate his wife's natural desire to have a child, she has no qualms over turning to her former lover, Jules Tonnerre, the half-breed Métis, who eventually fathers her daughter. In the world and milieu to which Morag belongs, she does not bear any stigma of immorality for bearing a child out of wedlock. But that kind of thing is absolutely unthinkable in the Oriental colonial setting of Bharati Mukherjee's novel. Tara, with all her emancipation and Western outlook, is horrified by the coarse joking of the middle-class Indian tourists she comes across at Darjeeling. Later her decision to cut short her visit to India is precipitated by a sense of shock over her unsolicited seduction by Tuntunwala, the industrial magnate, at the Nayapur Guest House. This highlights the vast difference between the two worlds of *The Diviners* and *The Tiger's Daughter*, the two worlds of the protagonists, Morag and Tara, who project the respective selves of the two colonial novelists, Margaret Laurence and Bharati Mukherjee.

NOTES

1. Margaret Laurence, *The Diviners* (Toronto: McClelland and Stewart-Bantam, 1973), p. 393.
2. Bharati Mukherjee, *The Tiger's Daughter* (London: Chatto and Windus, 1973), p. 36.

The Indian Middle-Woman in America: Cross-Cultural Concerns in Bharati Mukherjee's *The Tiger's Daughter* and *Wife*

More than twenty years ago Bharati Mukherjee, a Calcutta-born Indian girl, went to the University of Iowa in the USA to attend a two-year creative writing workshop. There she met Clark Blaise, a Canadian writer. They married after a short but intense courtship of six weeks. Thus began Bharati Mukherjee's dilemma, as she felt caught between two cultures of the East and the West. This conflict has constituted the main concern of her writings ever since. After getting her M.F.A. and Ph.D. from the University of Iowa, she went to live in Canada with her husband. There she lectured for some years at McGill University, Montreal, but writing remains her first passion. It was not easy, at first, to adjust to the Western way of life. And then, as she admits in an interview, for the first time in her life she encountered racial prejudice. She says,

> In Canada, I experienced an awful lot of racial discrimination—there were a lot of violent incidents in which Asians were roughed up—it was there in housing, in jobs. Canada was a very hard place to be a dark-skinned Asian in. After five years we moved to New York and I have never regretted that decision.[1]

Some of the bitterness felt by Bharati Mukherjee then and other cross-cultural concerns are projected in her creative writing. Apart from *Days and Nights in Calcutta*, which she wrote in collaboration with her husband, and which has been produced as a film, there is her great success, *The Middleman and Other Stories*, which fetched her the prestigious National Book Critics Circle award for fiction in the USA. An Indian woman married to a Canadian and now settled in the West, she declares that India remains a part of her past that she is proud of. But, at the same time, she believes her life is in the West—she feels herself to be part of the American literary scene. The initial problems of an expatriate Indian wife and writer in Canada are solved by recognition of her literary talent in the USA. This essay attempts an exploration of her dilemma, worked out through the fictional medium, in two of her early works.

Bharati Mukherjee's first novel *The Tiger's Daughter* (1971) and another entitled *Wife* (1975) concentrate on the cultural conflict of the East and the West. Each has a heroine of Indian origin, who suffers a culture-shock by going to the States. There is a similarity of approach to the main theme in both novels, but the author adds a touch of novelty in the second by reversing the position of the protagonist from that occurring in the first. Basically, both present an imaginative rendering of Bharati Mukherjee's personal experience in going West and the after-effects of the culture-shock felt by her personally. The point of difference is that while Tara, the heroine of *The Tiger's Daughter*, reacts mentally and physically to the changed scenario of a riot-torn Calcutta on returning to the city of her birth and early education, Dimple in *Wife* is a young Bengali bride, who accompanies her engineer husband to New York to face a way of life to which she cannot easily adjust. For Dimple, the shift from Calcutta to New York is a nightmarish experience, which finally leads her to an act that she could not visualize as a possibility under Indian conditions. It is obvious that Bharati Mukherjee has transferred her own cultural dilemma to the two heroines. The difference of approach in the two novels is also reflected by the names of the two women. One is called Tara, after a manifestation of the Goddess Durga, and the other bears the name of Dimple, a common Westernized Indian pet name. It is significant that *Wife* carries an introductory note, which gives the Oxford English Dictionary meaning of 'Dimple' as 'any slight surface depression.' The author is here hinting at the limited impact that her heroine has on the Indian community of New York.

The Tiger's Daughter is about Tara's return to India after seven years in the States, first as a student at Vassar and later as the Indian wife of her American husband, David Cartwright. David does not appear in the novel, but figures in Tara's reflections and her letters to him. His replies are her only link with America during her stay in India. Yet 'the American *jamai*' remains a strong bond with the East for 'the American auntie' of the nephews and nieces who greet her on arrival at the Bombay airport. The novel analyzes 'the anatomy of change,' the transformation of Calcutta from an oasis of peace and joy to the storm-centre of a political turmoil. Tara is surprised to find that so much could have changed—in just seven years—from the time when she was a carefree girl at the Convent of St. Blaise in Calcutta. She has to face riots and violence on the streets, daily processions of the factory workers, a virtual red revolution. It amazes and disturbs her at the same time. The complacence of Tara, the adored, beautiful and intellecutally-gifted daughter of Bengal Tiger Banerjee, a wealthy tobacco manufacturer, is so shaken as to put her nerves on edge. Even the company of her old friends, well-to-do young men and women, and their regular ritualistic visits for espresso coffee or tea to the Catelli-Continental Hotel on Chowringhee Avenue, are of no avail.

It is a new India that Tara rediscovers from the very moment of her landing at Bombay. All the fuss made over her by the Bombay uncle and aunt and their brood is expected enough, but the change in men's thinking and behaviour is apparent in the conversation of her two travelling companions on the long train journey to Calcutta. One of them is Tuntunwala, a middle-aged industrialist, who is repeatedly projected as a dynamic national celebrity and man of action. Eventually, it is Tara's seduction by this ugly yet fascinating man that precipitates her early return to America in spite of the importunities of her parents that she stay longer. The former St. Blaise and Vassar girl is subjected to all kinds of humiliations at Calcutta and Darjeeling that her refined sensibility meets with repeated shocks:

> From the roof of the Catelli, Tara saw Calcutta, squeezed horribly together, men, women, infants, some scratching their crotches, others laughing like tourists in an unfamiliar section of town. And always the heartbeat of the slogans. "Blood bath! Blood bath! Blood bath!"[2]

The Tiger's Daughter recounts the magnitude of a change that is mind-boggling in its dimensions. No wonder, Bharati Mukherjee comments early on in her novel: "Changes in the anatomies of nations or continents are easy to perceive. But changes wrought by gods or Titans are too subtle for measurement. At first the human mind suffers premonitions, then it learns to submit." (7)

The cultural shock to Tara, a Westernized Indian woman—Tuntunwala insists on calling her Mrs. Cartwright—is too big for her to bear. She has returned from America with high hopes of a fond reunion with parents, relations and friends of yore. She is eager to revisit her former jaunts, familiar streets and the Convent. But, at the end of the novel, she leaves for America in a hurry, almost surreptitiously, without taking leave of all her friends, suddenly informing her helpless parents about her decision "to return to David and the United States." Her resolve is preceded by gradual disillusionment with the Calcutta of her early youth. There are four important episodes that lead to the climax of her departure. The first of these is her visit to the burning ghats with an eccentric old man, Joyonto Roy Chowdhury, a tea estate owner, whom she meets at the Catelli. He decides to save her from the chaos surrounding the traditional way of life of his class in Calcutta, but in the process unwittingly administers the first serious shock to Tara's sensibility. The second episode is of the picnic organized by Tiger Banerjee at his factory premises for the entertainment of his daughter and her friends. A small snake is discovered in the swimming pool, where they frolic for some time before lunch is served. Tara is so horrified that she reacts by screaming loudly, which surprises even her parents. The third of her shocking experiences is at the summer resort of Darjeeling, where a group of middle-class Indian tourists behave rudely towards her when she goes out riding with her friend Pronob and English girl they meet at their hotel. The last straw is her seduction by Tuntunwala at the Nayapur Guest House, where she goes, at the suggestion of her father, to calm her nerves after the Darjeeling experience. That is when Tara finally decides to return to America. Her disillusionment with an India in upheaval is complete, and she concludes that it would not be possible for her—though born, bred and educated in Calcutta—to adjust to the changed conditions after her exposure to life in the West. Like her author, she too is a middle-woman caught in a cross-cultural turmoil.

Four years after the publication of *The Tiger's Daughter* appeared *Wife*, a novel in which Bharati Mukherjee considers the same problem from a reversed position and angle. Dimple is another Calcutta-born, college-educated maiden, whose marriage is arranged with Amit, a young Bengali engineer, who is ambitious of making a successful professional career in the States. Dimple too is enthused by same zest, as her husband does not care for a job in India. Her eagerness to go abroad is spurred on by the kind of drab and dull life she has to live at home in a middle-class household. Though her young brother-in-law gives her respect and company, the elderly mother-in-law does not appreciate Dimple's yearning for a more free life than she gets in a traditional Indian family. This is the trauma of most educated Indian girls, who have to suffer all the humiliations involved in an arranged marriage. The choice of a bride for a young man with a lucrative job is most humiliating for the girls he interviews one after another. This is the usual practice in an otherwise conservative Hindu society. The man has all the privileges and rights, but the poor woman is treated as a thing without feelings and emotions. She has to submit to the will of the man, the master, who treats her as a property that is worthwhile only so long as it provides pleasure and comfort to the owner. Brides are even today selected on the same basis. Bharati Mukherjee, being an Indian woman, knows about this directly, and reacts to it in her own way after her experience of the West. That is precisely the reason why she writes novels like *The Tiger's Daughter* and *Wife*.

Dimple and her husband ultimately land in New York. Amit is on the look out for a job, and stays with his friend. Jyoti Sen. Dimple tries her best to be of some use to her hostess. She helps in the kitchen and goes out shopping with Mrs. Sen. But it turns out to be a sad experience, as she does not know what to buy and how to ask for it at a store. The rebuff she gets in return is enough to discourage her from trying similar forays in future. In consequence, she decides not to venture out by herself again. But, in course of time, as Amit gets a foothold of a job, and they move to an apartment, which some American friends vacate for them, their life in New York moves on a different pattern. Now they attend parties and give parties, but all in the Indian circle of New York. This only strengthens the view how difficult it is for people of the Indian origin and background to adjust to the American way of life. The Durga Puja celebration that Amit's friends organize is expectedly an all Indian affair. There are, however, Marsha Mookherjee, an American woman married to an Indian scholar, and her brother Milt Glasser, who show some interest in the Indian community and its activities. Marsha's brother, further on, figures as catalyst in the surprise ending of the novel, but there are other concerns to be considered before we come to that.

Dimple, the obedient and faithful Indian wife, gradually loses faith in the ambitious dreams of success that Amit nurtures to the last. She is the first to realize that he is too spineless a person to succeed in the competitive economic jungle of New York. At the same time, she finds it is not so easy for a young woman like her, born and bred up in a totally different environment, to adjust to the American ways. The cultural and social gulf dividing the two worlds is too vast and deep for her to bridge over. The frustrations of her lonely and dull existence in the apartment, while Amit makes the rounds, looking for a suitable opening for a promising job, makes her depressed and neurotic. Over a period of several weeks, she contemplates nine different, fool-proof, methods of committing suicide. On top of this she feels neglected by her husband. The satisfactory love-life they enjoyed back home, in the early months of their married life, appears to her a long-forgotten dream. Amit, unfortunately, fails to appreciate his wife's hunger for love and care. The distance she finds herself at from her parents and college friends in Calcutta intensifies the situation. In desperation, Dimple virtually seduces Milt Glasser, to whom a casual sexual encounter with a woman he apparently admires is nothing unusual. But, because of her Indian background, it is quite a traumatic experience for Dimple, who feels transformed after her act of betrayal to Amit. It gives her enough strength to reject India and Indian ways by stabbing her unsuspecting husband in the neck. The great irony is that all the premeditation that has gone into Dimple's planning of nine ways of suicide finally bears fruit in her murder of Amit. This abrupt ending of *Wife* is Bharati Mukherjee's scathing comment on both Indian dreams of success to be achieved in the West, and attempts at adjusting to a culturally divergent life-style. Many Amits and Dimples in real life must have met the same fate as the two characters of her novel.

A comparative analysis of the fortunes of the heroines of *The Tiger's Daughter* and *Wife*, lead to some interesting conclusions. Both Tara and Dimple are projected as 'middlewomen' between two cultures, and both are shown as experiencing culture-shock in diametrically opposed conditions. Their disillusionment with India and America, respectively, is not sudden but gradual, over a period of time, and by stages. They take drastic steps at the end to get away from the cultural maladjustment that enmeshes them. The author's message is clear. The East or the West, whether she has had traditional Indian education or studied at a prestigious American institution like Vassar, the Indian woman, when facing an unfamiliar cultural environment, has problems that take unpredictable turns. No philosophy can help her under such circumstances. Having nothing and nobody to fall back upon, she has to tackle her problems by herself. Bharati Mukherjee is projecting a feminist point of view, that an Indian woman, caught up in a cross-cultural dilemma, has to be, ultimately, her own saviour.

NOTES

1. *Sunday* (21-27 May 1989), p. 76.
2. Bharati Mukherjee, *The Tiger's Daughter* (London: Chatto and Windus, 1973), p. 60.

An Interview with Salman Rushdie

In March 1983, shortly after he was awarded the Booker Prize for his second novel, *Midnight's Children*, Salman Rushdie came to India on a tour sponsored by the British Council. His itinerary included a two-day visit to Srinagar. He addressed the Faculty and students of the Department of English, University of Kashmir, and also participated in a seminar on *Midnight's Children*, held at the Government College for Women, Maulana Azad Road, Srinagar. Rushdie gave a reading from his novel, which was followed by the presentation of three papers on his book. Later, I availed of his presence by interviewing him for a broadcast over the Srinagar station of the All India Radio.

MLP Mr. Rushdie, I understand you have visited Kashmir often since your childhood. Your last visit was eight years ago. How do you feel on returning to the valley once again?

SR Well, basically, I feel very sad that I am here only for a day and a half, but I love coming back to Kashmir. It doesn't change, and you keep hearing the things that happen. Kashmir is Kashmir, and it is very nice to come here. I remember the last time I came—it was 1975. It was the last time I had been here for a long time, and before that I had been here as a child. My memories of Kashmir as a child were, of course, very wonderful, romantic, golden memories, and I was, in fact, quite nervous of coming back, because I thought maybe it won't really be as nice as I remembered when I was twelve or thirteen, and I thought it was going to be a let down and my memories would be damaged when I got here, but I discovered that it was, in fact, exactly as I remembered. There was absolutely no let down in the return. By then I was almost twice as old. So Kashmir is a special place for me, partly because of its beauty and partly because my family came from here.

MLP We are happy to hear your sentiments about Kashmir. *Midnight's Children* begins with a long episode that has idyllic Kashmir as its location.

SR Yes, it is a kind of figure of Paradise, and the novel begins in this pure, clean, simple, beautiful place. And when the grandfather leaves Kashmir, it has the feeling of a Fall, it has the feeling of a loss of that kind of innocence, or purity.

MLP Do you mean loss of Eden?

SR Yes, loss of Eden, and that was obviously Kashmir for various reasons.

MLP Mr. Rushdie, your third novel, *Shame*, in your own words, is a bitter account of Pakistan under military rule and dictatorship. Is Kashmir or any part of the sub-continent likely to figure again in any of your prospective books?

SR I don't know, I have no plans at the moment to write about Kashmir, but you never know. I mean I have, no doubt, no idea as to what my next two books will be. I just finished one, and at the moment my brain is having a rest. My feeling is that in the near future my writing will not be so much about India-Pakistan-Bangladesh, as about the experience of migrating from these countries to the West. That is something, after all, that I did and so many others have done, and so far it has been very little written about.

MLP We shall be very interested in reading your books based on your experiences in the West. But, for the present, what are your views on racism in England, your adopted country?

SR Well, there are only two views about racism. You are either for it, or against it, and, as for myself, I am against it. I think that one ought to put these things straight, that racism is not universal in England, and racism is also present in India. So let us not pretend we are without it. The thing in England is not the incidence of individual people being prejudiced against, which will be found anywhere in the world, but the feeling that some of the structures, some of the institutions of the society there are not fair and do not deal fairly between the races, of which the police forces are the most dramatic example. The odd thing about England is that the classic model of the race riots have never happened there, that is to say, it has never been the black community and the white community rioting against each other. That is not the way it happens. What happens is that it becomes, let us say, the immigrants against the police. That is the usual form, because there is a feeling that the guardians of the law and order are not guarding that community, and there is a great deal of justice in that feeling.

MLP What is your view of the state involvement with racial

prejudice?

SR I think the point about racism is that what one must fight is when it starts seeping into the institutions. I can understand there are people who do not like other people because of the colour of their skin, and I don't like them for feeling that way, but I can understand that it happens. I say the state must be free of that kind of taint.

MLP Are you against mixing racism with sports?

SR Do you mean banning South Africa?

MLP Yes.

SR Of course, we should ban South Africa from sports, because that is what hurts them. They are a country that is sports mad, and it is only because of the sports break that they actually notice that the world disagrees with them. And I don't believe you can separate these elements.

MLP Living in London, how do you feel about India?

SR Well, I think the place wherever you were as a child always has a special hold over you, and, until I was fourteen years old, I never left India. So it was my entire life until then. My family were here till I was seventeen, and so India represents a very large piece of me. I am not so much nostalgic as I have a feeling of remaining connected and not wanting that connection to be broken. I am not very nostalgic about India, but I keep coming back, and there are things in India which . . .

MLP But you are, at least, nostalgic about your boyhood memories.

SR Oh yes, I had lot of fun. I had a very nice childhood, which I have narrated in my book. My childhood was rather happy and content. So I remember that time also when Kashmir became a special place to me.

MLP You mean Bombay in the fifties and sixties.

SR The fifties and the first half of the sixties.

MLP I would like to know what you think to be the most suitable form of fiction today.

SR Well, if you are talking about India, which is probably most interesting, it seems to me the comic-epic is the natural form for India. Anyway, the great literature of India has been cast in the epic form, and the difference is that these days the idea of the strong man does seem to be the true portrait of the twentieth century man. So let us have comic epics instead of lyric epics.

MLP You mean in the tradition of Fielding.

SR I mean, yes, *Tom Jones* was the novel which invented that tradition—I mean the tradition of Fielding and his novel. And also, if you leave aside that tradition and begin the tradition, of Indian story-telling.

MLP *The Mahabharata* and . . .

SR Yes, and the old traditions. I remember, when I was at Baroda recently, a story-teller came to tell the *Mahabharata* story, and he drew a crowd of four lakhs of people, which shows what a great hold this form has, and I think it is important. As writers, we have to consider what kind of narration attracts the readers.

MLP Mr. Rushdie, please comment on the genesis and creative process of *Midnight's Children*.

SR I suppose it began as a family joke really; it began because of their being a joke in the family that I was born in June 1947, and two months later or slightly less than two months later, the British ran away [from India]. This joke was always told to embarass me at awkward moments, which gave me the idea to take a child and a country, and to join them comically. From that there was a short step to having the idea of a child that was born exactly at the moment of independence, and who believed himself to be connected to the country. Then, there was the story of the child growing up and the country growing up, so to say, in parallel—it began with that. For a long time I wanted to write a book about Bombay in the fifties and sixties, and that joined up with the other idea, and then stories and images began to come to me and speak together. That is how I told the Kashmir story in which there is this doctor and his patient who fall in love with each other.

MLP And the boatman, Tai?

SR Yes, the boatman was very important, because I wanted to have a kind of ageless and mythical character very near the beginning, who represented that part of India that was immutable and changeless. Tai is one of my favourite people in the book, and then the image of the doctor and his wife, or his future wife as they fall in love. That became very central to the book, that image, because the book re-uses that image in the later chapters.

MLP Would you like to say something about mixing history and fiction as you have done in *Midnight's Children*?

SR Yes, in the book I have discussed the relationship between private individual lives and public events. In the twentieth century it is still possible to get a situation in which characters, simply led by their interactivity with each other, bring about a revolution. A novelist is free to offer his own version of history in the guise of fiction.

Fantasy in Salman Rushdie's *Midnight's Children*

Fantasy is an inseparable part of the activities of the human mind. All individuals indulge in fantasy, whether it be about their love-life, economic position or public career. Freud's insistence on the psycho-analysis of human dreams is a tribute to man's capacity for fantasy. But for this escape valve, it would be hard for men and women to reconcile themselves to the harsh coldness of reality. There is no limit to the extent to which an individual's mind can go when its flair for fantasy finds a free rein. What is more, fantasy has been a very important feature of the literary activities of man. It is present in the folk-tales of all nations and races, in the major and minor classics of literature, and continues to inspire great writers to this day. You find it in the *Iliad* and the *Odyssey* of Homer, in the *Mahabharata* of Vyasa, and in the *Shahnama* of Firdousi. Even significant records of man's history sometimes make use of a touch of fantasy. When the historian cannot easily visualize an Alexander on the basis of mere facts, he may use his imagination to create the figure of a heroic soldier whose dream was to conquer the whole world.

Northrop Frye, in *Anatomy of Criticism*, does not discuss fantasy as a separate mode of creative writing, but he includes it in the mythos of summer, i.e., the romance mode. In his words, "the romance is nearest of all literary poems to the wish-fulfilment dream,"[1] which to my mind is nothing else but fantasy. After reading Salman Rushdie's *Midnight's Children*, I find it a delightful fantasy that makes selective and judicious use of history, which serves only as a background to the novel. Through his skill with words and mastery of language, Rushdie weaves dreams into reality, and blends truth and fantasy into an inseparable compound. The title of the novel is connected with Jawahar Lal Nehru's famous midnight speech, made on August 15, 1947, in the Central Hall of the Indian Parliament. "At the stroke of midnight" an independent nation held its "tryst with destiny," but Rushdie feels compelled to brood over the birth and future of a host of Indian infants born at the same hour and minute. The birth of a new nation is synchronized with the birth of several characters in the novel. The most significant among them is

Saleem Sinai, the central figure and narrator of *Midnight's Children*. The creation of this character and his midnight companions is a stroke of genius that lifts the novel out of the realm of history and autobiography into the higher world of fantasy, where sky is the limit.

Rushdie has woven fantasy into the very fabric and texture of his novel. Fantasy in *Midnight's Children* operates at three levels—verbal, episodic and structural. Verbal fantasy is an essential part of the style of the novel. Its purpose is to involve the reader into the magic web of words, and at the same time so to distance him from his environment that he is able to judge events and characters without a sense of personal involvement. I would not hesitate to add that verbal fantasy and the poetry of it achieve the same "estranging" effect that Brecht strives after in his plays. Dr. Aadam Aziz, boatman Tai, Ghani the land-owner and his daughter Naseem; Nadir Khan, Amina and Ahmad Sinai; Saleem Sinai himself, Shiva, Parvati and Padma—all are so caricatured and ironically treated that the reader feels alienated from each one of them, and yet drawn into the whirl of the story that he feels compelled to read on out of curiosity about their several destinies. That is exactly what Brecht hoped to achieve by his experiments with the epic theatre.

Midnight's Children is a fantasy spread over three books, divided into thirty chapters. Examples of verbal fantasy abound on each page. But to make my point, I would like to draw attention to Rushdie's art of the fantastic in Book One alone. Boatman Tai is described as "a watery Caliban." Naseem Aziz "could even dream her daughter's dream, just to know what they were getting up to." During a quarrel between husband and wife Dr Aziz's house at Agra, overcome with "the smell of silence," dwindles into a "bog of muteness." The British Cabinet Mission departs from Delhi in an atmosphere, where untouchables were being touched. Rushdie's central fantasy, round which the plot of the novel revolves, relates to the fact that "the baby Amina was carrying did not turn out to be her son." In the chapter called "Methwold," we have a parody of the transfer of power from the British to the Indians at the lower level of the transfer of possession of houses belonging to the Methwold Estate. It is described as a mere change of hands; everything is going to be the same down to the cocktail hour. As an illustration of verbal fantasy pure and simple, few passages of the novel excel the description of Dr. Aziz's nose:

> My grandfather's nose: nostrils flaring, curvaceous as dancers. Between them swells the nose's triumphal arch, first up and out, then down and under, sweeping in to his upper lip with a superb and at present red-tipped flick. An easy nose to hit a tussock with. I wish

> to place on record my gratitude to this mighty organ—if not for it, who would ever have believed me to be truly my mother's son, my grandfather's grandson?—this colossal apparatus which was to be my birthright, too. Doctor Aziz's nose—comparable only to the trunk of the elephant-headed god Ganesh—established incontrovertibly his right to be a patriarch. It was Tai who taught him that, too. When young Adam was barely past puberty the dilapidated boatman said, "That's a nose to start a family on, my princeling. There'd be no mistaking whose brood they were. Mughal Emperors would have given their right hands for noses like that one. There are dynasties waiting inside it,"—and here Tai lapsed into coarseness—"like snot."[2]

The detailed description is exuberently and coarsely humorous in the true Rabelaisian manner, and for ever imprints on the mind of the reader the gargantuan image of the formidable nose of Dr. Aziz. There is an echo of this message in Saleem Sinai's taking pride in being the "possessor of the most delicately-gifted olfactory organ in history."

The second type of fantasy that one encounters in the novel is of the episodic kind. Each of the thirty chapters describes a separate event or episode in the career of Saleem Sinai, beginning with the migration of his grandfather from Srinagar to Agra in the wake of his marriage to Naseem Ghanai. Each episode is a fantasy in itself, and also linked to the broader fantasy connected with the children of midnight led by Saleem Sinai. The children are all gifted with powers of telepathy. They communicate with each other over long distances; Saleem Sinai listens to their broadcasts at midnight like a wireless operator receiving signals from the radio stations all over the world. Each child has some distinctive and miraculous power of his or her own. Saleem can smell events long before they actually take place; Shiva is knock-kneed, but his knees are strong as clubs and with them he can knock off heads faster than an expert cook slicing carrots and onions for salad; Parvati, the witch, can work magical spells that place her in a class by herself. Here is all the paraphernalia of enchantment with which Rushdie creates episode after episode, soaked in the chemical compound of fantasy. To recall only a few among them, first of all, there is the wonderful account of the "Perforated Sheet" through which Dr. Aziz is, over a period of several months, allowed glimpses of different parts of Naseem Ghanai's anatomy depending on the nature and location of her several illnesses. As the novel progresses, the sheet acquires a symbolic significance of its own. "Hit-the-Spittoon" weaves a fantasy around the common Indian habit of betel-leaf chewing, which is a legacy from the nawabi culture of the Gangetic plains. "Commander Sabarmati's Baton" fantasizes the famous trial of Commander Nanavati, who was accused of murdering his wife's lover. Rushdie suggests that Saleem Sinai was a principal figure—behind the scenes—in that real-life drama that caught the imagination of the Indians for several months. "Movements performed by Pepperpots" transports Saleem to General Ayub Khan's dinner table, where he demonstrates a difficult manoeuvre that shapes the fortunes of the 1965 war between India and Pakistan. Similarly, the chapter entitled "Sam and the Tiger" is a fantasy involving the 1971 war, which resulted in the creation of Bangladesh as a separate nation, and in which General Sam Manekshaw played a vital role.

The element of fantasy, in all these episodes, is skilfully made subservient to the general structure of the novel, which develops the vaster fantasy. Rushdie makes it clear at the outset that the relationship between Saleem Sinai, the narrator, and Padma, the listener, is less of a physical nature, but more of an allegorical kind. *Midnight's Children* is a new *Arabian Nights* in which Saleem is to Padma what Scheherzade is to Prince Shaharyar. It is an acknowledgement of the changed times, values and circumstances that the roles are reversed in the present case; the man narrates while the woman listens, instead of the other way round. In the field of fantasy literature, no other work of man rivals the *Arabian Nights* for its richness, variety, breadth of scope, and quality of enchantment. It is a tribute to Rushdie's sense of the fantastic, and the quality of romance he is able to create in *Midnight's Children*, that we feel tempted to compare his art with that of the *Arabian Nights*. He spreads for us in his novel the magic carpet of the Indian capacity of retaining the traditional myths and creating new ones at the same time. While letting his fantasy-creating fancy roam freely across the pages of his novel, Rushdie also emerges as a myth-maker of considerable potential. That is a quality which is bound to make *Midnight's Children* an enduring classic of prose fiction.

The pull of the fantastic has always drawn the writers of fiction all over the world. It is a growing trend among the novelists of the twentieth century. Some of the living masters of fiction tend to discard absolute realism for myth and fantasy. In this context, I am reminded of the works of Aldous Huxley, George Orwell, William Golding, Gunter Grass and Kurt Vonnegut. Life today is become so complex and difficult that the traditional realistic novel no longer portrays it satisfyingly, either for the writer or for the reader. The contemporary writers are searching for ways to confront the world that is deprived of its living purpose. That is why, in the course of the present century, we have seen the emergence of such schools of fiction as the naturalists, expressionists, symbolists and absurdists. To be confronted with the truth about ourselves can be shocking, but mixed with a judicious dose of fantasy and enlivened by a touch of wit and gentle irony, it could be more palatable to the general reading public. Like several other novelists today, Rushdie provides a successful blend of realism and fantasy. In exposing our present state of corruption, he does not shock our sensibility, like a Swift or Pope, but drives home his point through a diverting narrative that, even when lapsing into the fantastic, is still rooted in reality. In the main he tells the truth, but it is memory's truth, which "selects, eliminates, alters, exaggerates, minimizes, glorifies, and vilifies also . . . in the end it creates its own reality, its heterogeneous but usually coherent version of events." (253) These words of Rushdie, quoted from the novel, successfully sum up the technique that he uses to create the world of fantasy and reality in *Midnight's Children*.

NOTES

1. (Princeton: Princeton University Press, 1971), p. 186.
2. *Midnight's Children* (Avon Books, 1982), p. 8.

The Writer as Historical Witness: Salman Rushdie's *Midnight's Children*

In March 1983, Salman Rushdie, the London-based novelist of Indian origin, was on a lecture tour of India. I had the opportunity of interviewing him for a programme. Among other things I asked him how the idea of writing a novel like *Midnight's Children* struck him first. He told me that it started as a family joke:

> It began because of there being a joke in the family that I was born in June 1947, and two months later or slightly less than two months later the British ran away [from India]. This joke was always told to embarrass me at awkward moments, which gave me the idea to take a child and a country, and join them comically. From that there was a short step to have the idea of a child who was born exactly at the moment of independence, and who believed himself to be connected with the country. . . . Then, there was the story of the child growing up and the country growing up, so to say, in parallel.[1]

I think all those interested in *Midnight's Children* as a work of fiction ought to take special note of this statement of Rushdie about the origin of the book.

Midnight's Children is a novel in Fielding's comic-epic-poem-in-prose tradition, in which fact and fiction come together. Rushdie believes that myths and facts of history are not always separate concepts, and could be made to substitute for each other. In his view, the paradoxes of history and those of private life have the same significance. If man loses the paradise of the future or utopia, he still has the paradise of the past, which is history. Today, novelists like Milan Kundera and Gunter Grass are re-inventing history. Their protagonists, the clowns, are the true inheritors of the new fiction. Rushdie acknowledges his debt to Kundera and Grass, and his Saleem Sinai, the narrator of *Midnight's Children*, belongs to their class of characters and fiction. It is a kind of fiction which attempts to re-write history. The facts of history that it unites may not be the exact events as they happened, because what Rushdie gives us is not the real truth but "memory's truth," which sometimes borders on the fantastic. A lot of what he writes in *Midnight's Children* is based on contemporary Indian history, though the twist that he gives it might create the wrong impression that he is taking all sorts of liberties with it. In this essay, an attempt is made to put on record straight by demonstrating how Rushdie uses historical material and why he throws a mantle of fantasy over it.

As a serious student of history, Rushdie believes that when history re-shapes itself through the imagination of a creative writer, it becomes a kind of fiction that can be as interesting and rewarding as any other form of the novel. Hence, he finds it difficult to keep history out of his literary work. This is clearly borne out by a close study of *Midnight's Children*, a socio-historical novel of our times. His problem, as that of several contemporary writers, in India and abroad, wanting to write such a novel about India, has been that of form. Rushdie finds a simple and original solution to the problem by synchronizing the births of his fictional hero and of independent India at the stroke of midnight of 15 August 1947. Through the device of locking together the destinies of the man and the nation, Saleem Sinai, like his creator, becomes a historical witness to the emergence of a new era in the history of a country. The process of the unfolding of the nation's annals runs parallel to the growth and development of Saleem Sinai from childhood to youth to adulthood. This provides Rushdie with a structural base from which he launches his character into intermingling planes of fact and fancy, history and fantasy. His exploration of the boundaries between history and fiction turns out to be a revision of real history. In fact, with his keen sense of irony, he provides a highly interesting alternative version of the official history. Rushdie writes about *Midnight's Children*: "What I was actually doing was a novel of memory and about memory, so that my India was just that: 'my' India, a version of all the hundreds of millions of possible versions."[2]

Rushdie compares his presentation of history to the pickling process, which preserves eatables and renders them tastier than in their original state to all kinds of palates. He pickles facts of history—a process that inevitably leads to change and transformation—for the noble object of preserving them for posterity. As Saleem Sinai says, 'To pickle is to give immortality.'[3] The generations of readers, contemporary as well as future, interested in the Indian history of the years immediately after independence, can whet their appetites by reading the spicy and pickled version in *Midnight's Children*. The metaphor of the writing of history in a framework of fiction as a kind of pickling is carried so far by Rushdie as to create the parallel of the Braganza pickle factory, which Saleem Sinai manages with the help of Padma and a wholly-female workforce. Padma is the hypothetical Shaharyar-type listener to the narrations of Saleem, a transformed Scheherzade in Rushdie's modern *Arabian Nights* (Saleem asserts that originally one thousand and one children were born all over India during the hours following midnight on 15 August 1947). In the last chapter of the novel, we are told of the thirty jars of pickle, corresponding to the thirty chapters of the book, standing upon a shelf, 'waiting to be unleashed upon the amnesiac nation.' (549) The thirty-first jar of the future is yet to be filled: "But the future cannot be preserved in a jar; one jar must remain empty—What cannot be pickled, because it has not taken place, is that I shall reach my birthday, thirty-one today." (550) Rushdie is aware of the limitations of his way of re-writing history, as is evident from this comment: "Sometimes, in the pickles' version of history, Saleem appears to have known too little, at other times, too much . . . yes, I should revise and revise, improve and improve; but there is neither the time nor the energy. I am obliged to offer no more than this stubborn sentence: It happened that way because that's how it happened." (549)

There are several ways in which Rushdie employs history for building the web of romance and fantasy in *Midnight's Children*. On the one hand, he provides us with perspectives of the past, mingling freely historical facts and truths of memory. On the other hand, he makes his hero participate in the creation of history, and uses events of history as references of time in the career of Saleem Sinai. The narrative takes off with an account of Saleem's grandfather in Kashmir in the early spring of 1915. For someone born in 1947, the gap of more than thirty years is to be filled, not from memory, but from the reminiscences of several characters. Here the author and narrator fall back upon some of the traditional ways of building history. It is in this part of the novel that perspectives of the past mix with the truths of memory borrowed from other minds. Expectedly, it becomes the reason for many discrepancies, far more than in the later part of the book. For instance, as a Kashmiri, I can vouch for the fact that the Dal Lake in Srinagar does not freeze over every winter, maybe on an average once in twenty years. But Saleem gives us a wrong impression in the opening pages of the novel that the freezing and thawing of the lake is a yearly phenomenon. Similarly, no Hindu women go up the Shankaracharya Hill in the cold severity of January to perform the rite of puja at the Shiva-lingam inside the hilltop temple. But Saleem has a readymade explanation of how he acts the part of an omniscient narrator: "Most of what matters in our lives takes place in our absence: but I seem to have found from somewhere the trick of filling in the gaps in my knowledge, so that everything is in my head, down to the last detail." (14-15) In the same context, let us consider his boast that, despite his Muslim background, he is quite well up in Hindu stories and myths. This declaration, unfortunately, comes in the wake of his erroneously attributing the scribe's role to the elephant-headed god, Ganesh, in the writing of Valmiki's *Ramayana*, instead of Vyasa's *Mahabharata*. But then there is his contention: "Reality is a question of perspective; the further you get from the past, the more concrete and plausible it seems—but as you approach the present, it inevitably seems more and more incredible." (197) With this bold assertion, Rushdie legitimizes Saleem's overlapping of history with truths of memory taken from the minds of a host of fictitious characters. Saleem's answer to the question of his true identity rejects all possibility of objection: "I am the sum total of everything that went before me, of all I have been seen done, of everything done-to-me. I am everyone everything whose being-in-the-world affected was affected by mine. I am anything that happens after I've gone which would not have happened if I had not come." (457)

Yet it is futile to censure Rushdie for taking liberties with facts of history as his Saleem has the sincerity to admit that the historian in him occasionally "fell victim to the temptation of every autobiographer, to the illusion that since the past exists only in one's memories . . . it is possible to create past events simply by saying they occurred." (529)

Now, let us turn our attention to how Rushdie re-creates history by making his protagonist participate in the process of history shaping itself. Instances of how it happens in *Midnight's Children* are multiple, but it is enough to pick out only a few significant examples of this kind to establish the point. On the very opening page of the novel, Saleem Sinai declares that he was born 'mysteriously handcuffed to history,' and later he became 'heavily embroiled in Fate.' 'Fate' is not an uncommon word to use in the context of the birth of an infant, but as the novel proceeds, we realize that it is not only the fate of an individual that is hinted at but also that of an entire nation. Rushdie synchronizes the birth of Saleem Sinai with the famous 'tryst with destiny' speech of Jawahar Lal Nehru, the first Prime Minister of independent India, who made that speech in the Central Hall of Parliament at midnight on 15 August 1947. Rushdie's hero and a new nation are born at exactly the same time, and hence the fates of the two are linked together. This invention in itself is a stroke of genius, and the rest of the novel follows as a sequence of events or history arising from that basic premise. The letter of the Prime Minister comes after the newspaper reports: "Dear Baby Saleem, My belated congratulations on the happy accident of your moment of birth! You are the newest bearer of that ancient face of India which is also eternally young. We shall be watching over your life with the closest attention; it will be, in a sense, the mirror of our own." (143)

Other extraordinary happenings follow this fateful birth. When sitting inside a huge washing chest inside the bathroom, a nine-year-old Saleem unwittingly spies upon his mother, the accumulated mucus of his prominent nose with upward thrust bursts through to the frontiers of the brain to bestow on him the power of telepathy, which makes it possible for him to tune into the thought channels of anyone he likes. In his narrative the adult Saleem comments on this discovery in these words: "at a crucial point in the history of our child-nation, at a time when Five Year Plans were being drawn up and elections were approaching and language marchers were fighting over Bombay, a nine-year-old boy named Saleem Sinai acquired a miraculous power." (204) The child Saleem immediately puts his gift into operation to probe and even change the course of history. One afternoon,

> I deliberately invaded the head of our own State Chief Minister, which was how I discovered, over twenty years before it became a national joke that Morarji Desai "took his own water" daily. . . . And finally I hit my highest point: I became Jawaharlal Nehru . . . and adjusted the Five Year Plan to bring into harmonic alignment with the music of the spheres. (207)

Shortly afterwards, Saleem crashes into history on a runaway bicycle. In other words, he meets an accident when he hurtles down the slope of a road to crash into the head of the first of the processions urging a linguistic division of the Bombay State. As a result of the jolt received in the accident, Saleem becomes suddenly aware of the one thousand other children born in India during the first hour of independence. For many years, he remains in telepathic contact with the surviving 580 out of them, for one hour daily, between midnight and one in the parliament of his brain. Later, during the Emergency under Indira Gandhi, they have a crucial role to play in the national history, and four hundred and twenty of them, including Saleem Sinai, are imprisoned together in Benaras. But before that, by yet another quirk of fate, Saleem goes to Pakistan, where he participates in the historic coup that imposes Martial Law in that country and instals General Ayub Khan as the unchallenged Dictator for ten years. The history of not one but two nations—India and Pakistan—is closely linked with the fate of Saleem Sinai and his family. He asserts: "Let me state this quite unequivocally: it is my firm conviction that the hidden purpose of the Indo-Pakistani war of 1965 was nothing more nor less than the elimination of my benighted family from the face of the earth." (403) By the same token, "the truest, deepest motive behind the declaration of a State of Emergency was the smashing . . . of the children of midnight." (510)

The narration of the story of Saleem Sinai, who finds himself mysteriously and mystically 'handcuffed to history,' is aided by allusions to historical events as references of the passage of time. The process begins long before Saleem's birth: "On June 4th, my ill-matched parents left for Bombay by Frontier Mail. . . . On the same day, Earl Mountbatten of Burma held a press conference at which he announced the Partition of India." (103-4)

Saleem's real mother, Vanita, is in a protracted unproductive labour on 14 August 1947. The first pangs hit her just as, hundreds of miles away, M.A. Jinnah announces the midnight birth of Pakistan. Even as Nehru says in New Delhi, 'At the stroke of midnight hour while the world sleeps, India awakens to life and freedom,' Saleem is born of Vanita at the Bombay nursing home. Out of a wrong sense of revenge, Mary the nurse, swaps this baby with that of Amina Sinai, born at precisely the same moment. That is how Saleem, the illegitimate child of Vanita and William Methwold, gets linked to history, and is brought up as the son of Ahmed and Amina Sinai. Two more instances would suffice to illustrate how the Sinai fortunes and the events of history march hand in hand on a parallel course in *Midnight's Children*. Saleem reveals that "after the death of my grandfather, Prime Minister Jawaharlal Nehru fell ill and never recovered his health. This fatal sickness finally killed him on May 27th, 1964." (334) Four chapters later, we are told: "My father was heading steadily towards his stroke; but before the bomb went off in his brain, another fuse was lit: in April 1965, we heard about the peculiar incidents in the Rann of Kutch." (398) These accidents ultimately led to the Indo-Pak war in 1965. As Saleem's fateful years roll on, the mill of history continues to grind.

Saleem Sinai is conscious of the tricks that his memory plays with him, when he puts pen to paper to write his or Rushdie's version of history. Re-reading his work, before the halfway stage, he confesses:

> I have discovered an error in chronology. The assassination of Mahatma Gandhi occurs, in these pages, on the wrong date. But I cannot say, now, what the actual sequence of events might have been; in my India, Gandhi will continue to die at the wrong time.
>
> Does one error invalidate the entire fabric? Am I . . . prepared to distort everything—to re-write the whole history of my times purely in order to place myself in a central role? Today, in my confusion, I can't judge. I'll have to leave it to others. (198)

In the last pages of the novel, he says: "To night . . . I reach the end of my long-winded autobiography; in words and pickles, I have immortalized my memories, although distortions are inevitable in both methods." (548) And again, "One day, perhaps, the world may taste the pickles of history. They may be too strong for some palates. . . . I hope nevertheless that it will be possible to say of them that they possess the authentic taste of truth . . . that they are, despite everything, acts of love." (550)

Salman Rushdie is a contemporary novelist, who is also a historical witness, if there is one. He finds it convenient to hide his personality behind his alter ego, Saleem Sinai, but the kind of fiction he dishes out in *Midnight's Children* has the unmistakable authentic flavour of history. Vast in its creative scope, spanning several decades of independent India's formative years, the book is more than a novel; it is virtual history. After the present analysis of this notable work of fiction that I have attempted, what could I say in conclusion? Let me say it in the words of Coral Ann Howells, who believes that Salman Rushdie re-writes history as protest. For her, *Midnight's Children* "is a deconstructive and creative re-working of history which supplements historical facts in order to give a more comprehensive account of historical process and of the continuum between lived experience and recorded history."[4]

NOTES

1. Taped conversation with the author.
2. Salman Rushdie, "The Indian Writer in England," p. 76.
3. Salman Rushdie, *Midnight's Children* (New York: Avon, 1982), p. 549.
4. Coral Ann Howells, "*The Temptations of Big Bear* and Salman Rushdie's *Midnight's Children*," *The Literary Criterion*, Vol. XX, No. 1 (Mysore: Dhvanyaloka, 1985).

Subversion of Faith as Fiction: Salman Rushdie's *The Satanic Verses* and Shashi Tharoor's *The Great Indian Novel*

Whether religion is divorced from politics or remains permanently married to it, there is no denying the fact that faith is an essential part of man's belief all over the world. Invariably, the question arises, what is faith? Is it blind or does it have a wide-open universal vision? Though it is said that there can be two sides to a question, this particular question has as many facets as there are people in the world. Across the world, we encounter confusing terms like *dharma* and *adharma*, 'belief' and 'non-belief,' 'theism' and 'atheism,' 'paganism' and 'Christianity.' The exact interpretation of these terms is always difficult, because of the individual preferences of the people attempting the almost superhuman task. But, whatever you say with regard to this puzzling issue, most people consider faith vital to their very existence. The Hindu concept of *dharma* is not just faith or religion, as it is commonly but mistakenly taken to be. Betty Heimann's definition as given in her book, *Indian and Western Philosophy: A Study in Contrasts*, and quoted by Shashi Tharoor in *The Great Indian Novel*, probably comes closest to the truth. She defines *dharma* as "total cosmic responsibility, including God's, a universal justice far more inclusive, wider and profounder than any western equivalent as 'duty'."

However these things are in men's individual estimations, it is an undeniable fact that the origin of literature has a very close link with religion. Poetry, in most parts of the world, was born of myth and legend, both having close links with some kind of belief or another. Two Indian epics, the *Ramayana* of Valmiki and the *Mahabharata* of Vyas, are as much parts of the Hindu belief as the *Bhagavad Gita*, a venerated religious book like the Bible of the Christians and the *Quran* of the Muslims. Similar instances of sublime poetry, in which gods figure as characters and participate in the affairs of men, are the *Iliad* and the *Odyssey* of Homer in Greek, and the *Aeneid* of Virgil in Latin. Examples of this kind are numerous, but all need not be enumerated here. However, a fact that deserves special mention relates to Greek tragedy, which evolved out of the ritual worship of Dionysus, and developed as part of the religious faith of the ancient Athenians. There could not possibly be a better instance of man's faith serving as inspiration for literature.

Taking a big leap across centuries, it would be noticed, from a purely conservative point of view, that there has been a general devaluation of arts, literature and culture in the twentieth century, especially after the universal trauma caused by the second world war. Disintegration of language as a medium of communication was projected in the Theatre of the Absurd. Subversion of faith as fiction, in these times, is perhaps symptomatic of similar trends in literature all over the world. The most talked about example of this is, undoubtedly, *The Satanic Verses* of Salman Rushdie. *The Great Indian Novel* of Shashi Tharoor is open to interpretation from a similar angle. Both the novels were published in the same year, 1988, which is just a coincidence, but highlights the importance of myth as inspiration and theme for creative writing even at the end of the twentieth century. Along with Rushdie's renowned though condemned book, I would like to focus attention on this literary phenomenon in the context of *The Great Indian Novel* of Shashi Tharoor. The author was born in London, grew up in Bombay and Calcutta, took a doctorate from Tufts University, USA, worked for the UNO, and happens to be a freelance journalist and writer.

Quite a few knowledgeable people regard *The Satanic Verses* of Rushdie a notable work of fictional art, as good as some of his earlier works, like *Midnight's Children*—which fetched him the Booker of Bookers Award—and *Shame*. It is an extremely well-written novel with a complexity of theme and design not often to be encountered in some of the pedestrian novels of today. But, unfortunately, these aspects of the novel tend to be ignored in the face of the fundamentalist hate campaign against the book by the Muslims all over the world. I must admit that most reviews and critiques of this novel that I have come across so far are coloured by the ominous shadow of the Late Ayatullah Khomeni's sentence of execution against Rushdie. This sentence hangs like the proverbial sword of Democles over the head of a talented writer, who has emerged out of the Indian subcontinent. This fundamentalist approach to *The Satanic Verses* is so narrow that it can only lead to a damning conclusion. One cannot but appreciate the democratic institutions of the United Kingdom, the then Prime Minister Margaret Thatcher—since dethroned—which granted Rushdie state protection that still continues. In this context, it should be noted that in the novel she is referred to as 'Mrs. Torture' and, worse still, as 'Maggie, the Bitch.' Indira Gandhi almost banned *Midnight's Children* for the reason that she had been called 'the Widow'—which she actually was—in that book. India has the dubious distinction of being the first state in the world to ban *The Satanic Verses.* I would prefer not to go into the compulsions that might have led Rajiv Gandhi, in 1988, into taking such a hasty step. But the fact remains, if we had not banned the book, perhaps the Iranian *fatwa* would not have followed. Rushdie is on record, in an interview in *The Times of India* of Sept. 10, 1993, saying how he feels about the whole sordid affair: "The rupture with India is what hurts me the most. . . . Pakistan always struck me as an insufficiently imagined community. . . . But to be expelled from India is very painful."

Most people, even after reading the novel, tend to forget that the story of Prophet Mohammed and the beginnings of Islam in and around the Mecca of fifteen centuries ago is only one of the themes of *The Satanic Verses.* Almost equal importance is to be attached to the plight of the racially segregated Bangladeshis, who sufer a miserable life in the London of the eighties of the present century. Theirs is a poignant story, comically but sympathetically told by a discrening observer, and touches the reader's heart. The continued racial discrimination against them and other Asiatics is a direct condemnation of the British police. Then there is the elaborate narrative of the villagers of Titlipur, led by a spiritually inspired Ayesha, on a foot-pilgrimage to Mecca. Fighting heavy odds all the way, they finally reach the Arabian Sea near Bombay. Most of them perish, engulfed by the waves, as they try to walk across to Mecca. But to the last, their faith in their leader and the hope of reaching their cherished destination remains undiminished. Two out of nine sections of the novel are devoted to this spiritually uplifting episode, which deals with 'faith' in a different manner from that in some other sections. For those who relish stories of romance and adventure in the New World, there is the gripping narrative of the Argentinian love story of Rosa Diamond and Martin de la Cruz, with its accessories of song and dance, spies, betrayals and assassinations. To the usual Bollywood buff, Gibreel Farishta along with his paramours, Rekha Merchant and Alleluia Cone, appears as a movie superstar in the mould of an Amitabh Bachchan and his escapades on and off the silver screen. In the heat and dust of the fundamentalist religious storm, one is likely to forget that Salman Rushdie is basically, what a successful novelist always ought to be, an excellent narrator, a teller of engrossing tales. There are few living writers of English fiction who could surpass him in this art. He demonstrates his skill to perfection in *Midnight's Children,* reproduces it in *Shame* and repeats again in *The Satanic Verses.* The great irony is that this book is more about citizenship and nationality than about Islam, for which it stands condemned.

This is not the occasion to discuss the framework of the novel, but one cannot overlook the broad outlook of the writer that emerges from a careful reading of the text. Rushdie's unequivocal stance towards his subject is satiric, of which irony is a principal ingredient. There is, then, his technique of allegorical parody, which envelopes both the theme and the structure. Let us not, here, go into the question of how authentic his facts are or what was the outcome of his research into the history of Islam, which he undertook as a graduate student at Cambridge. But the fact remains that he uses his knowledge of that study, and the commonly unknown facts gathered by him, in the fabric of *The Satanic Verses.* What bothers Rushdie is how the novel has become, as he says, "a peg for religious fundamentalism. I have never denied that *The Satanic Verses* is provocative, but provocation is not an excuse for murder, just as wearing a short skirt is not an excuse for rape."[1]

The question arises what is it that makes the novel provocative. What offends the Muslims is the author's satiric presentation of the beginning of the Mohammadan faith at Mecca or Jahilia, as Rushdie chooses to call the city in his novel. That term is not, perhaps, so offensive to the Muslims, as it only suggests the general atmosphere of ignorance prevailing in Arabia at the time when the Prophet first preached his message of there being only one Allah deserving of the worship of the Believers. What offends more is the medieval Christian name of 'Mahound,' with its derogatory connotations, by which Rushdie calls the Prophet. Then there is the question of discriminatory behaviour attributed to him in allowing a maximum of four wives to his followers, while retaining a harem of a dozen for himself. Exception is also taken to the satiric naming of twelve prostitutes of Jahilia after the twelve consorts of the Prophet. But the last straw is the suggestion that he was temporarily under the influence of Satan, when he publicly admitted to the divinity of three ancient goddesses—Lat, Mannat and Uzza—whom he was for a while ready to accept as daughters of Allah and, hence, venerable. To avoid unnecessary bloodshed and to secure powerful converts quickly, the Prophet is shown to be making this compromise. But, on second thought, he "announces the abrogation of the verses which Shaitan whispered in his ear. These verses are banished from the true recitation, *al-qur'an*. New verses are thundered in their place."[2] Prophet Mohammad is, thus, shown to be the recipient of a revelation in which satanic verses mingle with divine. This is, obviously, a subversion of faith that shocks the true believers, and enrages them against Rushdie. Apart from this, *The Satanic Verses* is an epic novel that takes the reader over a journey of laughter and tears towards the good and evil that are inseparably together in the minds of men and women. But the fact remains what is permissible in a liberal intellectual gathering may not go down well with people when their religious sentiments are cynically hurt for a loaded purpose.

The Great Indian Novel of Shashi Tharoor, in the author's choice of theme and its satiric treatment, certainly amounts to subversion of faith. The majority of the Hindus consider the *Mahabharata* to be religious literature of the highest order. *The Bhagavad Gita* containing the essence of the Vedas and Upanishads, forms part of the longest epic poem in world literature. Some of the most venerable names in Hindu myth, legend and belief figure as characters in this Indian classic. When Shashi Tharoor, in *The Great Indian Novel*, sets out not only to parody the grand epic, but also to lampoon its heroes, one feels that perhaps he is carrying the joke too far. But, then, his inspiration comes from P. Lal, on whose version of the epic, *The Mahabharata of Vyasa*, Tharoor depends most as a source book. Lal writes: "The essential *Mahabharata* is whatever is relevant to us in the second half of the twentieth century. No epic, no work or art is sacred by itself; if it does not have meaning for me now, it is nothing, it is dead." With this quote appearing ahead of even the table of contents, it sets the tone of Tharoor's novel, the title of which is an imaginative transliteration of the name of the original.

In retelling the well-known story, which is nearly 3000 years old, Tharoor deliberately devalues the religious sanctity of the original by referring to the sublime achievements of the grand heroes in terms of current language and idiom. For instance, Lord Ganapathi is described as a dim-witted stenographer employed by Vyad Vyas, the narrator of the epic, to take down his dictations. Telling the story of his life and times, Tharoor's Vyas declares unashamedly, 'I was born . . . a bastard . . the offspring of a fisherwoman seduced by a travelling sage.' What is suggested here is perhaps something that actually transpired, but the choice of words to put it in is, obviously, subversive. When King Vichitravirya dies childless, leaving behind his two widow queens, Satyawati, the Queen Mother, sends for Vyas to sleep with them in order to father heirs to the throne. She thinks, 'If he's anything like his father, he can certainly do the job.' (31) Vyas corroborates his mother's surmise, "And indeed I could. We Brahmin sons never deny our mothers, and we never fail to rise to these occasions. I rose. I came." (31) There is no need for me to explain the erotic puns, which are all too explicit.

Here, I must put in proper perspective the structure of *The Great Indian Novel*. Faithfully duplicating the eighteen *parvas* of the *Mahabharata*, Tharoor divides his novel into eighteen books, each bearing an imaginative title, taken from a well-known work with an Indian context.

A few instances should suffice: 'The Twice-born Tale,' 'The Duel with the Crown,' 'Midnight's Parents,' 'Darkness at Dawn,' 'Passages through India,' 'The Rigged Veda,' and 'The Bungle Book—or, the Reign of Error.' What is more, Tharoor wittily superimposes the structure of the *Mahabharata* on the history of the Indian freedom struggle and thereafter, hence, distorting the original text. In consequence, the heroic figures are burlesqued and caricatured as men and women of straw, who indulge in their various political games. Bhishma, the celebate stalwart of the *Mahabharata*, is renamed Gangaji, who bears a marked resemblance, in word and deed, to Gandhiji. Following the same comic-epic mode, the blind Dhritrashtra is visualized as a power-hungry Jawahar Lal Nehru, Pandu is Subhash Bose, Vidur is Sardar Patel, Yudhishtir is Morarji Desai, Drona is Jaya Prakash Narayan, and Karna is Mohammed Ali Jinnah, who succeeds in carving out his cherished Karnistan out of the original undivided kingdom. The Kaurava clan represents the powerful Congress party, the great divide which is brought about by the machinations of Priya Duryodhani, who is none else but Indira Gandhi. Draupadi symbolizes various entities at different times in the retold epic, but she is obviously 'democracy,' very much at stake in the great gambling match and the subsequent *dharma yudha* at Kurukshetra. In this manner, there is plenty of spiced fare, to each according to his or her taste, for the contemporaneous readers of Shashi Tharoor. I, for one, am particularly intrigued by the account of Maharaja Vybhichar Singh of the northern state of Manimir, when he is coerced into signing the Instrument of Accession by the official emissary of the Government of Hastinapur.

Even Lord Krishna is not spared by the satiric pen of Tharoor. He is described as a local MLA and the Kaurava party secretary for a remote *taluk* in Kerala. On first meeting Arjun, during his enforced wanderings, Krishna imitates Ishmael in Melville's *Moby-Dick*: "'Call me Krishna.' The party secretary smiled. 'Everyone does. Dwarakaveetile Krishnankutty Parthasarthi Menon is a bit of a mouthful even in these parts.'" (327) When both Yudhishtir and Duryodhani seek his support before the onset of the battle, which is projected as an electoral contest, Krishna says, "One side can have me, alone, not as a candidate, with no party funds, but fully committed to their campaign; the other can have the massed ranks of my party workers, disciplined and dedictated men and women." (392)

The Satanic Verses of Rushdie and *The Great Indian Novel* of Tharoor are easily comparable at two levels: at the thematic level of subversion of faith, and in terms of their structural complexity. In addition to the central historical core of Prophet Mohammad's Mecca and the gradual spread of his message, *The Satanic Verses* deals with a multiplicity of themes that highlight the tragedy and comedy of man today in different parts of the world. Intentionally or unintentionally, Rushdie might have inflicted pain and outrage on people of his own faith, but that should not detract from the overall artistic excellence of a well-written work of fiction. It does not deserve to be rejected outright. One needs to look at it from a broad philosophical Hindu point of view that is capable of accommodating criticism of matters relating to faith and belief. Rushdie has an uncanny gift of fantasy and myth-making, rarely encountered in contemporary English fiction. At the same time, his felicity of juggling with language and ideas is widely recognized. As in his other works of fiction, no less in *The Satanic Verses*, he remains a skilful and masterly craftsman, who builds this epic novel with careful attention to layer upon layer of intermingled narratives.

The Great Indian Novel of Shashi Tharoor is a comic retelling of the *Mahabharata* story, into which the author cleverly interweaves the fate and fortunes of the players of the never-ending comic drama of modern Indian politics. His witticisms of language and caricature of characters are fitted into the ready-made structure of an epic poem that in its original sweeps across worlds of romance, faith, belief and philosophy of life. Tharoor tends to be discursive and repetitive, if only in his attempt to parody the enormously wide range of the original. *The Great Indian Novel*, at best, amuses the curious reader, and might lose its topical interest after some time, but Rushdie's unjustly damned book will be perused again and again, if only for an individual analysis of grounds for the sentence of execution that still hangs over his head.

NOTES

1. *The Times of India*, Sept. 10, 1993.
2. Salman Rushdie, *The Satanic Verses* (London: Viking, 1988), p. 124.
3. Shashi Tharoor, *The Great Indian Novel* (New Delhi: Penguin Books India, 1989), p. 19.

Salman Rushdie's *The Moor's Last Sigh*: Yet Another Controversial Novel

Salman Rushdie is a writer who thrives on controversy. First, it was with *Midnight's Children* which narrowly escaped being banned in India by the Indira Gandhi government, in 1983. Second, it was the turn of *Shame*, which was assailed in Pakistan. Next, it was *The Satanic Verses* which was first condemned and then banned in India under the Prime Ministership of Rajiv Gandhi. The great irony was that not many people, who bitterly attacked the book, had actually read it. And, now, it is happening to Rushdie's latest novel, *The Moor's Last Sigh*, which was initially banned in parts of India without a legitimate reason for such an outrage. At this rate, every other cartoon of R.K. Laxman is likely to be banned in the near future. India is an independent country, where freedom of expression is constitutionally guaranteed. Yet, it is such a pity that curbs on this fundamental right of the people are exercised from time to time for wrong reasons.

Over the years, one has come to associate the appearance of each new Rushdie novel with some controversy or another. Such an outcome could not always be deliberate, pre-planned or intentional on the part of the author. The anticipation of the reading public as well as the advance publicity provided by the mass media are equal contributory factors in this recurring phenomenon. For instance, but for the advance publicity, there was no reason why *The Moor's Last Sigh* could not be released in Bombay, in 1995, when it was sold all over the world. Even in Delhi, the book-sellers did not display it openly, but, out of caution, sold it under the counter. The mere fact that one minor character—Ramon Fielding—has some resemblance to the Shiv Sena supremo, Bal Thackeray, is not a sufficient reason for banning the book than a dog being named Jawaharlal, a writer's gimmick that should have offended most Indians. Even if the caricature of the Shiv Sena Chief were intentional, there are features in the character of Fielding that have no resemblance whatsoever with the mannerisms and political practices of Bal Thackeray.

The title of Rushdie's novel is connected with two paintings of the same name made by two different characters. The first is actually a portrait of Aurora Zagoiby, the mother of Moor, painted long before the birth of her son.

On being rejected by her husband, Vasco Miranda, the artist paints over it the figure of the last Arab Sultan sadly leaving Alhambra on the back of a white charger. Vasco calls it 'The Moor's Last Sigh.' Later on, as the culmination of her 'Moor sequence,' Aurora paints an unfinished portrait of her son, which she calls by the same name as Vasco's earlier painting. Both these paintings are stolen from Bombay, and Moor discovers the two together, at the end of the novel, at the Castle of Vasco in the Spanish village of Benengeli. Incidentally, a third painting—an actual one—has joined the two of fiction. It is called 'Salman Rushdie: The Moor,' and was painted by Bhupen Khakhar, in 1995, for the BBC. The painter has this to say about Rushdie and the painting: "When I met him for his portrait, he was in great spirits. He had just finished *The Moor's Last Sigh* and there was the likelihood of the *fatwa* being lifted. I painted him as the Moor with a club hand, in profile, like in Moghul miniatures. I have painted Bombay on the left and characters from the book are on both sides of the portrait."[1]

The Moor's Last Sigh is a mixed kedgeree of various aromatic ingredients. It starts simmering at an odorous house on Cabral Island near Cochin, and comes to boil at *Elephanta* on the Malabar Hill in Bombay. The hot spices and other elements are provided by the antecedents and growth of two clans. The Portuguese Da Gamas are the maternal line, while the Jewish Zogoibies are the paternal line, out of the Union of which emerges Moraes Zogoiby, also known as Moor, the protagonist of Rushdie's novel. Aurora Da Gama, his mother, combines artistic genius with her acumen for handling business. Abraham Zogoiby, the father, is equally good in the sphere of trade and commerce, but towards the end of the novel he surprises every one, including his son, by turning out to be a mafia boss of the stature of an actual Dawood Ibrahim. These three, along with Vasco Miranda, a small time painter, who rises to acquire an international reputation through his patronage by and association with Aurora, are the central figures of Rushdie's novel. There are a host of minor characters who drop in and out of the story at regular intervals as the main plot progresses from Cochin to Bombay and onwards to Spain.

Worthy of note among the lesser characters are Camoens and Aires Da Gamas, father and uncle of Aurora, and Isabella and Carmen, her mother and aunt, whose contrasting personalities provide the spice of interest in the early chapters of *The Moor's Last Sigh*. Epifania is the eccentric old grandmother who drives a teenage Aurora to desperate rebellion. Abraham's mother, Flory Zagoiby, unsuccessfully tries to prevent her infatuated son from marrying a younger but fiery Aurora. She brings some elements of mystery from her Spanish background into the early part of the story. Then there is Lambajan Chandiwala, the one-legged gate-keeper of *Elephanta*. With a talking parrot parched on his shoulder, he is an obvious imitation of Long John Silver, the pirate in R.L. Stevenson's *Treasure Island*, the perennial children's classic. The peculiar name of the gate-keeper is a fanciful invention of Salman Rushdie, who is very adept at coining puns out of Hindustani-English combinations. It is Lambajan who rescues Moor from jail, where he is incarcerated on an alleged charge of narcotics smuggling and the murder of Uma. Ramon Fielding or Mainduck, the frog-like cartoonist turned Mumbaiya Axis, M.A. for short, a political party that gains control over Bombay. Moor first works for him, and later kills him before running away to his Spanish exile. Ina, Minmie and Mynah, the three elder sisters of Moor, do not have much to do with the progress of the plot, but they are there merely as the female siblings of the chief protagonist of *The Moor's Last Sigh*. Equally superficial, as the very names suggest, are Nadia Wadia, the beauty queen, and her mother, Fadia Wadia. Who knows what associations these funny names have in the childhood memories of Salman Rushdie. Uma Sarasvati, the art student from Baroda, has some role to play in shaping the destiny of Moor during his last days in Bombay. Though the two of them become lovers, she shocks him by betraying him to his parents.

Aurora Zogoiby, Moor's mother, beautiful and brilliant, passionate and rebellious, is a forceful figure and at the centre of the various movements of the plot. She begins early as an astute business woman at Cochin, where she takes charge of the spice trade of the Da Gamas. Later, at Bombay, she pursues her unusual talent for art. There she comes into contact with some of the contemporary artists and intellectuals of her time. None of the men in the novel come up to the stature of Aurora, who is a multi-faceted personality. In this saga of the two families, Moor projects her as a kind of Mother India figure, after the famous role of Nargis, the Bombay actress, in the celebrated film of Mehboob Khan. In this very context, the narrator reflects, "Motherness . . . is a big idea in India, may be our biggest: the land as mother, the mother as land, as the firm ground beneath our feet."[2] About the times spent in the company of Aurora, he has this to say:

> my joy in life was born in our collaboration, in the intimacy of those private hours, when she talked of everything under the sun, absently, as if I were her confessor, and I learned the secrets of her heart as well her mind. (221)

And here is the comment on the Moor series of paintings done by her on the subject of her son: "I was happy to be there, because the story unfolding on her canvases seemed more like my autobiography than the real story of my life." (227)

Abraham Zogoiby, Aurora's colourless and dull husband, is no match for her. Nor for that matter is Vasco Miranda, the flashy painter with the Salvador Dali moustache. We are told that the source of his indefatigable activity is the needle in his blood-stream, which will one day reach his heart to end his life. The needle is symbolic of the hopelessness of his love for Aurora that does not let him rest in peace. His final encounter with Moor seems a sort of contrived affair, though it is the culmination of the immediate events leading to it. Vasco Miranda's 'Indian Variation' upon the theme of Einstein's Theory of Relativity makes interesting reading: "Everything is for relative. Not only light bends, but everything. For relative we can bend a point, bend the truth, bend employment criteria, bend the law. D equals mc squared, where D is for Dynasty, m is for mass of relatives, and c of course is for corruption, which is the only constant in the universe." (272) His fondness for fantasy and imaginary world corresponds to that of his creator. One of Rushdie's fantasies in the novel is to bring together from different historical periods writers like Premchand, Sadat Hasan Manto, Mulk Raj Anand and Ismat Chugtai into Aurora's drawing room for a literary chat with her. Obviously, these are some of the favourite writers of Rushdie himself, and they connect him with the Bombay of his own boyhood. Incidentally, when Moor praises *Mother India* as a film and disparages *Mr. India* by contrast, he only reflects the author's preference for the one and rejection of the other.

Rushdie's novel is 'A Moor's tale, complete with sound and fury.' (4) Narrating the tale is a compulsion for Moor, much like that of the Ancient Mariner of Coleridge, a way of expiating his sins. 'Life itself being Crucifixion enough,' (4) especially because of the *fatwa* still hanging on his head like the sword of Damocles, Rushdie himself, in his fugitive state, has an overpowering compulsion to unburden his mind, to tell the story as and how it transpired. A special device of Rushdie in narrating the events of the plot is to project Moor as a man in a great hurry, tearing along the road of life to reach the end of his journey. He is born only four and a half months after conception (half of the normal time), and after the passage of twenty-one years, he is already a middle-aged man of forty-two, a young man in an older man's skin. Perhaps this is the trick of the psychology of a writer, who is forced by circumstances to lead an underground existence. In this context, Moor makes an unusual confession: "I grew in all directions, willy nilly. My father was a big man but by the age of ten my shoulders had grown wider than his coats. I was a skyscraper freed of all legal restraints, a one-man population explosion, a megalopolis, a shirt-ripping, button-popping Hulk". (188)

As in his other works, in *The Moor's Last Sigh* too, Rushdie has a special concern with purely Indian themes, and provides in it echoes of actual news items that have something to do with India. For instance, he mockingly refers to the idea of a secular definition of spirituality, and mentions Majority (for Hindus) and Major-Minority (for Muslims) in the context of the Indian political scene. Then there is a clever juxtaposition of Ganesha-puja in Bombay and outbreak of the plague at Surat: 'Indian rats, as we know, carry gods as well as plagues.' (123) The Zagoiby mansion at Malabar Hill is named *Elephanta* after the island in the Arabian Sea off the port of Bombay. The Indian version of MTV is given the title of *Masala Television*. On the bomb explosions and consequent outbreak of communal clashes in Bombay, Rushdie comments from the depth of his heart: "the explosions burst out of our very own bodies. We were both the bombers and the bombs. The explosions were our own evil—no need to look for foreign explanations, though there was and is evil beyond our frontiers as well as within." (372) But at less sad moments, he recalls South Indian meat with Coconut milk, Mughlai Kormas, Kashmiri Shirmal, reshmi kababs, Goan fish, Hyderabadi brinjal, and even pink salty numkeen chai that is rarely known outside the State of Jammu and Kashmir.

Rushdie's on-going love-affair with Bombay, the city of his birth, is as much evident here as in two of his earlier novels, *Midnight's Children* and *The Satanic Verses*. Before the *fatwa*, he was a regular visitor to Bombay, not only for collecting notes for his books, but also because he likes to be on the streets of his favourite city. It is evident from the way he loves to mention by name the famous landmarks of Bombay: Malabar Hill, Chowpatty, Marine Drive, Colaba, Nariman Point, Mahalaxmi Race Course, Breach Candy, Juhu, etc. His Moor does not fail to mention even the places of tourist interest in the vicinity of Bombay. It is with a rare sense of nostalgia that he recalls the names. "Mahabaleshwar, Lonavala, Khandala, Matheran. . . . O cool beloved hill stations I will never see again, whose names echo for Bombay folk with the memory of childhood laughter, sweet love-song, and days and nights in cool green forests, spent in walking and repose!" (142)

It is apparent that Rushdie feels homesick for the city where he lived for the most impressionable of his childhood years. After the Zagoibies leave Cochin, it is Bombay all the way for them and the readers until Moor escapes to Spain as much in search of a sanctuary as looking for the lost 'Moor paintings.' The two middle sections of the novel, 'Malabar Masala' and 'Bombay Central,' which form the bulk of the book, are both located in Bombay, while the first, 'A House Divided,' belongs to Cochin, and the last, 'The Moor's Last Sigh,' takes Moor to Benegeli in Spain. The Indian readers of Rushdie know that the satirical columnist 'waspyjee' is a pseudonym for 'Busybee' of the *Mid-Day*, an afternoon paper of Bombay. In chapter 18, one comes across another dimension of the city: "Bombay was central, had been so from the moment of its creation . . . all rivers flowed into its human sea. It was an ocean of stories, we were all its narrators, and everybody talked at once." (350)

Rushdie is not a philosopher, but offers history in the form of pickled fiction. One does not go to him to seek a world-view or to be educated on what is good or bad for one in life. If some readers discover loaded messages in his works, those are only incidental to his main concerns. Rushdie is such a popular writer for the sheer fun and entertainment that he consistently provides; he rarely disappoints the expectations of his readers. He is a kind of magician who dexterously plays tricks with language, characters and real life situations. His penchant for punning and coining ever new expressions and turns of phrase in Indian English of the Bombay variety keeps his readers, especially in the Indian sub-continent, perpetually amused. At Cochin, in Aurora's words, 'it was pepper first and one most—yes, yes, onemost, because why, say foremost? Why come forth if you can come first?' (5-6) The three clerks at the Da Gama warehouse are mischievously named Kalonjee, Mirchandalchini and Tejapattam. Expressions like 'lettofy' and 'maddofy' are too numerous to be all listed here, but 'hit-fortune' as the opposite of 'mis-fortune' is too quaint a turn of phrase to be passed over without mention. Similarly, there are 'hit-take,' 'hit-alliance,' 'hit-conception,' 'hit-terious,' etc. And, the last but not the least, here is this classic Indian English structure from what one Indian gossip is overheard saying to another: 'You samjao that baysharram pair.' (97) Could anything beat the mixed flavour of such a funny piece of conversation?

NOTES

1. Bhupen Khakhar in conversation with Rani Dharkar, *The Sunday Times Review*, March 31, 1996.
2. Salman Rushdie, *The Moor's Last Sigh* (London: Jonathan Cape, 1995), p. 137.

Wole Soyinka: A Witness of His Times

There was a time when writers—poets, dramatists and novelists—were valued more for universality than for their contemporary relevance. Homer and Virgil, Chaucer and Shakespeare, Kalidasa and Firdousi are still read for the enduring qualities of their works, whether these lie in their epic structure, narrative skill, dramatic art, descriptive skill or in the panorama of life that they unfold in different languages and literary forms. We treasure their creative writings for the pleasure they afford to people of all ages, generations, races and nationalities. A rose is a rose in whatever colour or form it comes before us, and so is a piece of literature, whatever age or language it belongs to. John Ruskin, the Victorian writer, in his lecture entitled "Of King's Treasuries," distinguishes between books of the hour and books for all time. By the former, he means journalistic kind of writings, while the latter include all classics of a permanent value. Such thinking has ruled the domain of literary criticism for several centuries. But today the trend is changing, and a writer's commitment to his own life and time is valued as much as his universal appeal.

Currently, readers all over the world look for both permanent values and contemporary relevance in the writers of their choice. This is particularly applicable to those who write in the recently liberated and still developing countries of Asia and Africa. Today, the vast majority of the African blacks judge the worth of their writers on the count of how significant their contribution is to the African resurgence and in highlighting the problems of the much-exploited black race. In this context, the work of Wole Soyinka, sometimes called the Black Orpheus of Nigeria, is of great importance.

Soyinka is better known as a playwright and poet than as a novelist. But he was awarded the Jock Cambell New Statesman Award and the Nobel Prize for Literature, 1986, chiefly on the strength of his novel, *The Interpreters*. Born at Abeokuta, Western Nigeria, in 1934, he was educated at the colonial Nigerian schools and the university of Ibadan before he went abroad to the university of Leeds in England. He followed it up by doing a short stint as a play-reader and script-writer at the Royal Court Theatre of London, and thus gained professional experience as a man of the theatre. Soyinka returned to Nigeria in 1960 to work, one after the other, at the Ibadan and Lagos universities. At the same time, he made efforts to revive the Nigerian theatre much on the same lines as Yeats and Synge did for the revival of the Irish theatre at the beginning of the twentieth century. Soyinka was imprisoned at the outbreak of the Nigerian civil war in 1967, and released in 1969.

The literary achievements of Wole Soyinka are outstanding. Soon after joining the Royal Court Theatre, he wrote his first plays in 1958—*The Swamp Dwellers* and *The Lion and the Jewel*—which were first produced in London and later presented at the Arts Theatre, Ibadan. *A Dance of the Forests* and *The Trials of Brother Jero* followed in 1960. *The Road* had its premiere at the Theatre Royal, London, in 1965. Most of these plays had revivals later at different theatres in London. The internationally acclaimed play, *Kongi's Harvest*, was first presented at Lagos in 1965, and one year later it was produced at the First World Festival of Negro Arts at Dakar. Apart from these plays, Soyinka published half a dozen collections of poems and two novels, *The Interpreters* (1965) and *The Season of Anomy* (1973). *The Man Died* (1972) is an account of his experience in jail.

Wole Soyinka is a writer with a strong sense of commitment, and he has had a quick rise to fame. He is equally committed to his work and the reading public for whom he writes. Only twenty-three when his first plays were staged in London and Ibadan, within a few years he won recognition as the leading African dramatist. But during his twenty-six months in prison he composed only a few short poems. This dark period marks a definite break in his career, both as writer and as man of the theatre. The first hectic decade of his literary activity is clearly marked off from his later mellow phase. Today he is in the middle of another creatively fruitful period. Soyinka writes realistically as well as symbolically about the events that are shaping the contemporary history of Nigeria and other African states. His interest is fixed in the colonial days of the immediate past and the struggles of the newly independent nations to stand on their tottering legs. Like Chinua Achebe, that other great Nigerian writer, he is a witness of his time.

Soyinka does not often talk about his work in detail, or of the deep experiences of life on which it is based. But his writings are so clearly linked with the events of his own life and time that the critics feel compelled to associate the two. Gerald Moore, in his book entitled *Wole Soyinka*, relates each work of the Nigerian genius to his total activity in the theatre and in society at the time of its conception. The productions of *The Swamp Dwellers* and *The Lion and the Jewel* at the Arts Theatre,

Ibadan, in February 1959, were a revelation to the Nigerian audience. Moore writes: "Here, only two years after the construction of the first proper theatre in the country, was an African dramatist who could people its stage with credible characters and fill their mouths with an English unmistakably local in its full-blooded ebullience. Clearly, Wole Soyinka must be brought home as soon as possible. . . . In the early months of 1960 Soyinka landed at Lagos with the early drafts of two new plays already in his pocket and a decade of intense creativity for the Nigerian theatre had begun." (9)

A Dance of the Forests is a tragic play that combines elements of the Elizabethan masque and Brechtian narration with those of the ancient ritual and tradition of the Nigerian folk-dance. Like *The Tempest* of Shakespeare, it was written to celebrate a joyous occasion—in this case the significant event of Nigerian independence. Soyinka brings together in this play the idea of 'The Gathering of the Tribes,' and the idea of a divinely-ordered confrontation between certain mortals and their historical prototypes of a distant age. The sets and costumes for the play were designed by the young Nigerian artist, Demas Nwoko; the important double role of Obaneji and Forest Father was played by Soyinka himself. The character called Half-Child represents, among other things, the destiny of Nigeria, to be saved at independence by a change in the hearts of men. The play is addressed to the regeneration of man rather than to any earthly political concept which ignores man's unchanging nature.

Soyinka's tragic plots centre round a death, and attempt through their action to evaluate that death for those who survives. Thus, he restores to the word 'tragic' its proper significance: tragic death is not an ordinary passing away but an event full of deep meaning for the community that witnesses it. This is clearly borne out by *Kongi's Harvest*, which is Soyinka's comment on the contemporary political scene in Africa. The death of Segi's father in this play causes an upheaval in the state, but it is not the upheaval that the writer hoped for, because the play ends on a question-mark. Its fairly elaborate typicality is a defect in *Kongi's Harvest*. Certain phrases and attitudes of fashionable dictatorship are already less familiar than they were twenty-two years ago. But a careful recasting of a few lines might serve to revive the play for a later generation of spectators. This defect to which attention needs to be drawn only strengthens the point of view that Soyinka is a witness of his time, if there is one in the present-day Nigeria.

An important work of Soyinka that must be mentioned here is his first novel *The Interpreters*, published in 1965, the bumper year in his literary output. In this complex and rich novel, he takes a critical look at the human situation in modern Nigeria. There is a great deal of incidental satire in the exposure of shallow men with their phoney attitudes towards everything. People talk callously about moral issues while totally ignoring the human predicament of those involved. The novel is built round an epic structure. It starts in the middle of the affairs of the main characters, a group of six young intellectuals, endlessly reflecting on the individual and collective life in Nigeria. Sagoe is a journalist, Bandele and Kola are university lecturers, Egbo works at the foreign office, Sekoni is an engineer and sculptor, and Lasunwon is a lawyer. All of them are professional men trying to make their careers, enjoying the good things of life and influencing the public affairs of their country. Their great virtue lies in their determination to think for themselves. They are the outspoken interpreters of life in post-independent Nigeria, and as good witnesses of their times as Wole Soyinka, the man who created them.

The Interpreters is an attempt to bring Soyinka's tragic vision of African life within the compass of a novel. Like everything else that he writes, it tries to achieve what he declares in his paper on "The Writer in Modern African State" as the chief objective of writing: "It seems to me that the time has now come when the African writer must have the courage to determine what alone can be salvaged from the recurrent cycle of human stupidity." That is a criterion equally applicable to all writers anywhere in the world today.

Chinua Achebe's *Things Fall Apart* and Wole Soyinka's *The Interpreters*: A Comparison of Narrative Techniques

Today, the leading lights of Nigerian literature are undoubtedly Chinua Achebe and Wole Soyinka. The two literary giants are still carrying on the tradition of Nigerian writing, though the first was born in 1930 and the second followed four years later. Achebe broke fresh ground in 1958 with the publication of his first novel, *Things Fall Apart. No Longer at Ease* (1960), *Arrow of God* (1962) and *A Man of the People* (1966) followed in close succession. With these four novels, a collection of short stories and an anthology of poems, by 1972, Achebe established himself as a writer of vision known not only in Nigeria and Africa but all over the English-speaking world. In 1975 appeared *Morning Yet on Creation Day: Essays* that revealed a new aspect of the Nigerian genius—his educational and critical interest. Achebe's novels are an ironic comment on the stages of transition in the colonial world during the past one hundred years. In the words of Christopher Heywood, "Achebe is never a mere reporter of public events. He rejects the view of the writer as one who writes either for his own professional pleasure or for the sake of merely reporting events in the external world. He also rejects the over-facile views of history, based on misreadings of evolutionary doctrines in the nineteenth century, which have prevailed until very recent times. Instead his novels affirm permanent moral and social values as they emerge in detailed moments of crisis in the lives of individuals and communities."[1] In addition, Achebe is a deeply committed writer, who focuses the attention of his readers on the social and political history of his country during the century preceding Nigerian independence. His declared aim as a writer is to teach and educate.

Wole Soyinka's rise to fame was more spectacular than that of Achebe. He too has a sense of commitment to his work and the audience for whom he writes. It is significant that he burst on the literary and theatrical world in 1958, the year that witnessed the publication of Achebe's first novel. His chosen field of activity is the theatre as against the world of fiction where Achebe secured his due recognition. Only twenty-three when his first plays were staged in London and Ibadan, within a few years, Soyinka came to be known as the leading African dramatist. He wrote *The Swamp Dwellers* (1957), *The Lion and the Jewel* (1957), *A Dance of the Forests* (1960), *The Trials of Brother Jero* (1960) and *Kongi's Harvest* (1965). All these plays were presented both at London and in Nigeria. Soyinka himself directed and acted in some of these. His rise to fame in Africa and the commonwealth countries was phenomenal. Today, he is fifty-three and in the middle of another fruitful period. Besides the plays, he has published several collections of poems and two novels, *The Interpreters* (1965) and *Season of Anomy* (1973). He won the Nobel Prize for Literature in 1986, and the citation made special mention of *The Interpreters*.

Things Fall Apart and *The Interpreters* are both first novels of their respective authors, but there is a big difference between the two. While Achebe had published nothing before his novel, Soyinka had established himself as a poet and man of the theatre before experimenting with the novel form. Achebe was perhaps just learning his craft, whereas Soyinka was already a great literary innovator on the stage. If Achebe's novel is a beginner's first assay at writing fiction, *The Interpreters* of Soyinka is the work of a confident and mature author. It is interesting to investigate how the two Nigerians set about the challenging task of handling what was for them a new form of writing. In this context, this essay attempts a brief comparison of the narrative techniques of the two novelists.

First of all, let us examine the common features that link these novels together. Achebe and Soyinka have almost identical backgrounds. Both had the advantage of the same kind of education at the colonial schools and colleges before they started writing. Both are teachers at the University level—one of literature, the other of the theatre. *Things Fall Apart* and *The Interpreters* are both first novels establishing the reputations of the authors as masters of fiction. They have similar concerns in attempting to explore the clash of traditional and new values in a transitional African society. Hence the relevance of a comparison between the two novels.

In *Things Fall Apart*, Achebe presents new subject matter to the Nigerian and Commonwealth reading public in a literary form borrowed from Europe. He uses several modes of narration, and also has recourse to the traditional Igbo and African way of telling the story of a tribal hero, Okonkwo, who is tragically destroyed and his community humiliated at the end of the novel. In the opinion of Christopher Heywood, "The story is built up from a point of view closely related to that of the culture being portrayed. The ceremonials marking the seasons, the birth, life and death of individuals, their urges of feeling in moments when the social order is threatened and the ties of religion and kinship which knit the community together are shown with scrupulous, affectionate fidelity. Each ceremony or custom forms an essential part of the delineation of character." (7)

At the same time, Achebe seems aware of the narrative arts of the classical tragedy and epic, and draws from these European literary forms. *Things Fall Apart* is a tragedy told in the epic manner. The omniscient author mediates between the action and the reader. The narrator's intrusions to comment on an episode or character connect Achebe's novel with Homer's epic tradition.

Elements of both praise-poem and lamentation are the interesting features of *Things Fall Apart*. It is an elaborate praise-poem deemed to be recited by a member of the class, such as Obierika, Okonkwo's friend. At the end, it is Obierika who speaks in anger to the District Commissioner, whose intervention precipitates the tragedy: "That man was one of the greatest men in Umuofia. You drove him to kill himself; and now he will be buried like a dog."[2]

The central preoccupation of the novel is a lamentation for the past glories of the traditional Igbo society and an appraisal of Okonkwo. There is a fair sprinkling of fireside grandmother tales, such as those of Vulture (38), Mosquitoe (53) and Mother Kite (98-99). These gain depth from being told in situations which relate to the destiny of men and women of Umuofia and, in turn, complement the narration. The hero's exile from and return to his native village are reminiscent of the *Odyssey* of Homer and *Oedipus Rex* of Sophocles. Yet the novel retains its basic African character, which points to Achebe's originality as a writer.

Soyinka too is influenced by the European literary forms in his narration of *The Interpreters*. He successfully employs the epic device of starting in the middle of the affairs of his main characters. They are a group of six young Nigerian intellectuals reflecting endlessly on the individual and collective life of their country. Soyinka does not narrate the story in the chronological order of the events, but moves freely backwards and forwards in time for filling in the pictures of his characters that emerge in the novel. Eldred Jones, in his Introduction to *The Interpreters* puts it succinctly: "The reader must be prepared for these changes in time or he will make nothing of the novel. . . . Soyinka gives us a vivid picture of Sekoni the newly qualified engineer, as he leans on the deck of the ship that is bringing him home dreaming of how he is going to transform his country with his engineering skill." (26-27) Then without a break he is swept from the height of his imagination to his office desk and shown performing humdrum tasks like signing bicycle permits and vouchers.[3]

This style of narration gives the novel compactness of structure and lends an epic dimension to it. Another device that helps the epical design is Soyinka's deliberate use of poetic language and imagery. There are passages in the novel that have echoes of Soyinka's poems. For example, Sekoni's death in a car crash is described in a manner that reminds one of the poem called 'Death at Dawn': "Sekoni's body lay surprised across the open door, showers of laminated glass around him, his head one fastness of blood and wet earth." (155)

Similarly, Egbo's first sexual encounter with Simi is presented through poetic imagery (60) rather than through stark description. For that matter, the entire novel is an extended metaphor. Soyinka achieves the complex effect of projecting the points of view of several characters, who are the interpreters of contemporary Nigerian society.

The similarities between *Things Fall Apart* and *The Interpreters* can be multiplied, but there are some points of contrast between the techniques of the two novelists that need to be pointed out. Both make use of poetic devices, such as imagery and fable, but Soyinka's commitment to the art of the poet is greater. Achebe's narrative draws on the traditional African story-teller's art, and his language and structure are comparatively simpler. But Soyinka achieves greater complexity of technique and form by following the tradition of the modern European novel. There is, however, a touch of originality even in his borrowings, for he demonstrates with authenticity the moral and religious values of the Igbo tribal culture. *The Interpreters* is a great African novel that provides insight into a developing Nigerian society. Achebe needed to write four novels in order to project the same concerns.

NOTES

1. "A Critical View on Chinua Achebe's *Things Fall Apart*" (The Nexus Series, London: Collins in association with the British Council, 1985), pp. 3-4.
2. Chinua Achebe, *Things Fall Apart* (Singapore: Singapore National Printers, 1985), p. 147.
3. Wole Soyinka, *The Interpreters* (London: Heinemann, 1970), p. 2.

West African Tribal Society in the Novels of Elechi Amadi

Among the contemporary Nigerian writers in English, three novelists have gained prominence as masters of fiction. Chinua Achebe provides in his novels an analysis of the conflicting political and social issues in the Nigerian life. John Munonye examines the cultural clash between the traditional and modern way of life. In contrast to them, Elechi Amadi concentrates on faithfully presenting the traditional tribal society of West Africa, untouched by the white man's culture. This essay attempts to examine this aspect of his fiction by a close look at his three novels: *The Concubine* (1966), *The Great Ponds* (1969) and *The Slave* (1979).

Elechi Amadi deliberately chooses to write of a time before the arrival of the Europeans in his country to present an authentic picture of the tribal world, not savage but noble and ordered, and far removed from the white man's world. The currents of disorder come to surface in the tribal village community only when the gods are wronged, but there are proven ways of placating each angry god. While presenting the life in the West African villages still governed by the gods, Amadi also depicts the delicate human relationships for that society.

In *The Concubine*,[1] the first of his novels, Amadi uses Nigerian folklore as the structural basis for his story of misplaced love. The mystery of the successive deaths of the lovers of Ihuoma of Omokachi village is explained as her being the incarnation of the favourite wife of the Sea-god, who causes the destruction of any man who approaches her sexually. Working within this mythical framework, Amadi describes the functioning of the village community. We come to know the elaborate process of negotiating for a bride, from the first visit of the groom's party to the girl's house right up to the escorting of the bride to her husband's house. Amadi also writes in detail about the day-to-day life of the villagers—planting, harvesting and marketing of yams; the fish trade; the trapping of wild animals; the extension of compounds and thatching of roofs; and the ritual singing and dancing on occasions of joy and sorrow.

The first of the lovers of Ihuoma to die is her husband Emenike. In a fight initiated by his rival, Madume, Emenike gets badly hurt in the chest. Gradually his condition worsens and he finally dies. Madume hates Emenike for having married Ihuoma, and deliberately way-lays him on the forest track to pick a quarrel with him. But the possibility of killing his rival fills Madume with fear, because "the cost of the rites of purification was prohibitive and even after that he would still be a branded man." (3) Some time after Emenike's death, Madume goes blind when a cobra spits poison into his eyes, and he commits suicide. The third of the lovers of Ihuoma to perish is the youthful and generally admired Ekwueme. He too comes under the spell of the graceful woman. Though his parents arrange his marriage with a pretty young girl, Ahurole, he finds it more and more difficult to forget Ihuoma. Ahurole goes back to her parents, but not before having administered to her husband a powerful love potion which her mother gets from a dibia or witch-doctor. Ekwueme becomes insane, and the only one who can handle or pacify him is Ihuoma. In desperation, his parents consent to Ekwueme marrying the woman of his choice, but he dies after being accidentally hit by an arrow shot by a child killing lizards. All these happenings are related to the central structural myth of Ihuoma being the incarnated wife of the Sea-god. The framework helps Amadi to reproduce the traditional tribal way of life in authentic detail.

Under the economic conditions prevailing in rural Nigeria, yam-planting is very important to the villagers. Apart from being their staple diet, yams are also a source of income as the surplus yield is sold in the market. Yams and cocoyams are to be planted in their proper season, and need care from time to time for a rich harvest. Men and women share this responsibility equally. If, in a certain household, there are not enough people to do all the work, neighbours and friends help at the time of planting and harvesting. There are fixed market days when the excess produce is sold, and fish, cloth, utensils and other requirements are bought in exchange. Some men, like Ekwueme, are not interested in farming, but make good hunters. They fix their traps in the forest close to the village to catch rabbits, fowls and wild boar. It they are lucky, sometimes they catch a deer or an antelope, the flesh of which is greatly relished by the villagers. It is the routine of the hunters to visit their traps every morning in the hope of finding a catch. Similarly, others make the rounds of their palm trees for tapping palm wine.

Besides being a favourite drink of the people, palm wine is offered along with the kola nut at formal occasions, at rituals, and when negotiating for a bride. For example, at the time of making arrangements for Ahurole's wedding we are told: "Ahurole was engaged to Ekwueme when she was eight days old. Ekwueme was then about five years old. The initial ceremony was simple. Ekwueme's father, Wigwe, merely put some kola nuts and the shoots of young palm wine saplings into the vessel from which Ahurole drank. Thereafter he kept an eye on her casually. Nothing was done beyond this until the children were of age." (98-99)

Wigwe believes that a father's primary duty to his son is to get him a good wife. So he dissuades Ekwueme from marrying Ihuoma, a widow with children, and opens negotiations with Ahurole's father, Wagbara of Omigwe village. It entails several visits to the bride's house, extending over many months, and repeated gifts of palm wine. On the first occasion, Wigwe, Ekwueme and two of his friends go, carrying only one calabash of wine. Wagbara entertains the party with foo-foo of pounded yam. Ahurole helps her mother in serving the guests, and Ekwueme finds an opportunity of observing her at leisure. At the end of the meal, when palm wine is served, Wigwe informs Wagbara that he has come to ask for permission to begin negotiations for a marriage between their two children. Wagbara grants the permission, and appoints his younger brother to be Wigwe's guide during the negotiations. After the first visit, many more journeys to Omigwe are made. "They accomplished very little on each occasion but it cost them no small amount of money. For one thing they carried three kegs of palm wine on each subsequent visit: for another Ahurole's relations were by no means few and many of them were entitled to something from them." (121)

Finally, the day for the formal 'presentation of wine' arrives. This time Wigwe is accompanied by the village elders. They are all neatly dressed in gay wrappers and sing their way to Omigwe. Wine carrying is expensive on both sides. The calabashes are returned to the groom's family after this great occasion. The bride goes to stay in her husband's house for four days before returning to her parents. Six months after the start of negotiations, Ahurole is finally escorted to live with her husband in a separate house in the family compound. In her case it is a quick marriage, as the normal period of negotiations is a year.

In the world of Amadi's fiction, the young people live their life of passion, love and activity, but the old people too remain busy with their own concerns. Ihuoma holds her husband's second burial rites shortly after the new yam festival, as it is a convenient time for feeding the great number of people who attend the ceremony. "Early the next morning the old women began to troop in. Each carried a small bag neatly folded under her armpit. These bags would later house goat-meat and other delicacies which the women would take back to their children and grand children. No mother would go to a feast and fail to bring 'parcels' home to her children, no matter how small her share might be." (32)

The old women are served with dried meat in palm oil sauce. They chat and gossip, and munch huge chunks of meat offered to them. After the old women, it is the turn of the young men, friends of the dead man. They sing and dance, chant and stamp their feet in unison. "Here was a dance of passion, a dance of anger, a vehement protest against the god of death, an appeal for the recall of their departed comrade." (33) They are served with gin and palm wine, and at night fed with foo-foo, soup and chicken.

Dibias are not all of the same class. Each has his own strength and style. It is reflected in the manner of their divination, the remedies and sacrifices prescribed by them, and the efficacy of their magic. Anyika of Omokachi is a good enough dibia on the basis of his achievement and reputation. But some villagers think his charges are too high. Others are of the view that he is not capable of countering the more vicious evil spirits. Anyway, he is not able to fight Ekwueme's mental disturbance. In desperation, his father sends for Agwoturmbe: "Agwoturmbe the dibia arrived with a great flourish. He had yellow paint round one eye and white paint round the other. He walked with a swagger which made his small round belly appear bigger than it was. He carried no knife or other weapons but everyone knew he was adequately protected. Behind him trotted a small boy carrying his medicines." (206) Agwoturmbe instructs Wigwe how to make arrangements for a special sacrifice to tame the Sea-god. But the gods have their own ways of frustrating human designs. All the items for sacrifice are assembled, except a brightly coloured lizard, which is easily found in the village itself. The task of getting one is left to a boy, whose arrow, directed at a lizard, accidentally finds Ekwueme as its mark. Ekwueme's tragic end concludes *The Concubine*, Amadi's moving account of the fate of Ihuoma's lovers.

Amadi's second novel, *The Great Ponds*,[2] deals with a serious clash between the tribal communities of two villages, Chiolu and Aliakoro. The bone of contention is the Pond of Wagaba, each tribe claiming the sole rights of fishing in its waters. The endless quarrel causes the destruction of more than half of the populations of each village. The tribes are led by their respective chiefs, who follow the time-honoured rituals and customs strictly. Of special interest are the sounding of the ikoro as a signal for a communal gathering and the elaborate negotiations for settling ransom or dispute. The tactics adopted by the two tribes for vanquishing each other in the prolonged conflict include camouflage, deception, and the use of magic and witchcraft. The dibia, naturally, enjoys a prominent position in the tribal society of this novel.

The great leader who sustains the people of Chiolu in the prolonged conflict is Eze Diali, an elderly man of great courage, experience and wisdom. His job is not to take part in the actual fighting, but, like a modern military commander, to plan the moves, assign duties to men and women capable of carrying them out, and handle the negotiations in such a manner as to secure the maximum advantage for his tribe. In all these respects, Eze Diali is an astute and capable chief, who, in the tactical battle, proves more than a match for Eze Okebi, the leader of Aliakoro. Diali has human qualities which make him greatly respected in his own village and by the other chiefs. Whenever there is sickness or death in some family of his tribe, he is the first to call on the stricken household, to offer consolation, help and condolence. He takes care of the funeral rites and rituals that follow a death. His dedication is particularly commendable when he continues to do his duty towards others even after the great epidemic spreads to his own house.

The people of both the villages are highly superstitious, and make frequent use of magic and witchcraft to help them in their difficulties. It is a common practice to wear special amulets for protection against dangers. This aspect of the tribal society is borne out in the person of Olumba, the Chiolu warrior, whose fate becomes involved with the central concern of the novel. When the people of Chiolu met for the first time to discuss how to counter the poaching by the men of Aliakoro at the Pond of Wagaba, "Olumba removed a small black amulet from his neck and substituted a bigger one. The former was for general protection at home, the latter for protection and luck while travelling. Ready at last he picked up his matchet and headed for the chief's house." (8)

Olumba has a small room adjoining his reception hall. It houses costly images of gods and very powerful charms. His three wives are forbidden to enter this medicine chamber. He possesses a special amulet that is supposed to deflect arrows aimed at the wearer. Similarly, there are other amulets which are reputed to make the wearer invisible. However, all these defenses are of no avail, when Igwu, the dibia of Aliakoro, works very powerful magic to destroy Olumba's sense of self-preservation. Olumba's continued good health is important to Chiolu as, at a joint assembly of the warriors of both the tribes, he has sworn by Ogbunabali, the god of the night, that the Pond of Wagaba belongs to Chiolu. The traditional time limit for such an oath is six months. If he survives this period, the gods would be understood to have decided the issue in favour of Chiolu. But in case he dies, it will be a victory for Aliakoro. The elders of Aliakoro plot and scheme for the destruction of Olumba. They even persuade Igwu, against his wishes, to work towards that end. Fortunately, Eze Diali is able to procure the services of Awuanwu, a highly reputed dibia of a distant village, who checks the evil effects of Igwu's spells. Olumba survives to make sure the Pond of Wagaba remains with Chiolu. But this triumph is achieved at the cost of great personal anguish, and loss of his eldest wife and daughter through sickness. His favourite wife, Oda, is kidnapped and his only son, Nchelam, is subjected to much suffering by the evil efforts of magic.

Eventually, the great endurance and sacrifice of Olumba is set at naught by the final act of Wago the leopard-killer, the renowned champion of Aliokoro. He is the owner of three leopard skins, which he has acquired by killing the beasts single-handed. Wago is a good wrestler, an unyielding fighter, who has the nasty temper of a wounded leopard. Throughout the conflict with Chiolu, it is he, and not Eze Okehi, who sustains the perseverance of the people of Aliakoro. With his belligerency and influence on the young warriors, he forces his people to continue the fight for the Pond of Wagaba against heavy odds. There is a feeling of personal rivalry between him and Olumba. They have several clashes in night encounters and by daylight, but are somehow unable to eliminate each other. When Olumba has virtually secured the pond for his tribe, Wago nullifies his great effort by drowning himself in it, thereby making it useless for his enemies, for Eze Diali says at the end, "It would be an abomination to fish in a pond in which someone committed suicide." (192)

There are two other aspects of the novel which deserve consideration. First, there is the great devotion of the women towards their menfolk and the self-effacing service that they render to their families. If a man has more than one wife, there is little feeling of rivalry or jealousy among the co-wives. In fact, they live together as sisters, and their prime concern is the comfort of their husband and the welfare of the common brood of children. It is remarkable how Nyoma, the first wife of Olumba, cares for Nchelam, the son of his third wife, when the latter is kidnapped by the men of Aliakoro. In a male-dominated tribal society Nchelam has special importance in Olumba's household as the only son among his children. This fact is accepted unchallenged by all the women of his family. When Olumba's enemies want to exert pressure on him, it is this very child who becomes the target of their magical practices.

Secondly, there is the spread of the mysterious epidemic that does not respond to traditional cures, and takes a heavy toll of young and old lives not only in the two villages, but also across the whole of West Africa. The tribes regard it as a visitation of the anger of the gods, and are helpless against its ravages. It cows them down as no beast, man or spirit would. They call it wonjo, and compose sad songs about it:

> Children are motherless,

That is what wonjo has done;
Maidens are now widows,
That is what wonjo has done;
Wonjo the curse of the gods,
Wonjo will end the world. (185)

Wonjo is the name the villagers give to the Great Influenza of 1918, which claimed twenty million lives all over the world. Incidentally, the reference to this world-wide epidemic indicates the time of action of *The Great Ponds*.

The Concubine focuses attention on the communal life of a tribal village in West Africa at the beginning of the twentieth century; *The Great Ponds* elaborates the theme of the inter-tribal conflicts; *The Slave*[3] deals with a new subject: the life and aspirations of the youth. It is the story of Olumati, who returns from exile to live in his ancestral home at Aliji. He was bred up in another village, where, after a feud with the Okani family, his father had taken refuge at the shrine of the god Amadioha. The people of Aliji find it difficult to accept Olumati as one of them, but he makes serious efforts to adjust himself to his new surroundings. Eventually, he is forced to go back and become the slave of Amadioha. In the process of narrating the story of Olumati, Amadi also describes the elaborate ritual of a maiden entering and coming out of the discipline of 'mgbede' before her marriage. The tender friendships of young girls are sensitively presented by the author. Another feature of the tribal life described in detail is the wrestling of the young men in which the entire village community participates.

Even as he enters Aliji for the first time in his life, Olumati meets Enaa, a graceful young maiden of the village. He is impressed by the charm of the girl, whom he knows to be a close friend of his sister, Aleru. From that very moment he cherishes the desire of some day marrying this paragon of grace and beauty. The witty exchanges of dialogue between the two young people is of special interest in the novel. Having decided to live in the village of his forefathers, Olumati tries his best to get on well with the entire village community. His cantankerous grandmother, Nyege, who never left the ancestral home, manages to get the approval of Minikwe, the village chief. Still, Olumati does not have an easy time in his new environment. When the grandmother dies, Aleru continues to look after his household till she is married to Nyeche, and even after that. Later, he is on his own. He learns to cultivate his fields some of which are already occupied by his enemies. It is a lesson in endurance when we read of how he teaches himself the art of tapping wine from the palms, which he sells for a living. Later, he astonishes everybody by displaying his skill at wrestling. He has a rival in Aso, who covets his lands as well as the girl he loves. By throwing Aso in the wrestling arena, Olumati is able to neutralize his evil intentions, but he cannot help losing Enna to Wizo, a carver, who does not carry the stigma of being a slave of Amadioha.

Of equal interest with the fate of Olumati in *The Slave* is Enna's entering 'mgbede' which is a social ritual perhaps unique to the West African tribal society. There is hardly any parallel to it in the oriental world. Amadi describes it in detail: "Mgbede, Erekwi girls were thrilled by it. In fact, all it meant was that at puberty a girl was given a long holiday before she took on the burdens of marriage. Mgbede could be as short as six months for girls of poor parentage or as long as two years. While in mgbede a girl's mother taught her the secrets of marriage, if, as was usually the case she was already engaged to a man, mgbede gave her a chance to study and assess her future husband before setting up house with him. An engagement could be broken during mgbede, though this was rare." (11)

Wrestling is an important feature of the life of the tribal society. All young men are expected to take keen interest in wrestling matches. There is a fixed season for the demonstration of the physical prowess of the various champions. When a particular tribe organizes a wrestling festival, stalwarts from other tribes and villages also participate. The organizer provides the arena and arranges the drummers without whom a wrestling match is impossible. The main bouts are generally preceded by the wrestling of the children. The sport is so popular that even girls indulge in it, but late at night when men are not present. The tense atmosphere on the eve of a wrestling match is faithfully captured:

> Women cooked feverishly as the drums throbbed. Wrestlers cleaned their wrestling dress and decorations and strengthened wrestling amulets and concoctions. A whitish soupy preparation was considered particularly important. Rubbed across the eyes it warded off the effects of aju, a charm that could induce staggering.
>
> The day is old,
> Your foes are here,
> Throwers of men,
> The drums call you. (106)

In these three novels, Amadi presents the tribal society of the past before the coming of the Europeans to Nigeria, which no longer exists in its unadulterated purity, and with the passing of which have also passed the old West African beliefs and values. While all the three novels provide a complete picture of that ancient traditional culture, each of them focuses attention on some special aspect of that way of life. *The Concubine* portrays the elaborate and protracted negotiations for a bride. It might appear a tiresome process, but a man will certainly value a bride won in this manner. The entire process is geared to make for a solid and long-lasting marriage. It also dispels the mistaken notion that the African tribals were ravagers before they came into contact with the Europeans.

Amadi's portraiture is, however, not of pure adulation. In *The Great Ponds* he dwells on an unpleasant feature of the tribal life: a long-drawn conflict between two villages over the matter of fishing rights in a stretch of water. We also get to know how superstitious and magic-minded these people are. If *The Concubine* gives a glimpse into an ordered but sorrow-ridden society, *The Great Ponds* reveals that their griefs are partly of their own making and partly a result of their supernatural practices. The only calamity that comes from outside is 'wonjo' against which the people are utterly helpless. *The Slave* is the story of a few individuals, very sensuously and sympathetically told. Besides the fate of Olumati, which is the chief concern of the novel, it enhances our understanding and appreciation of two important aspects of the West African tribal society: 'mgbede' and the wrestling matches. 'Mgbede' is a well-conceived practice that aims at helping the young maidens to mature, mentally and physically, before they take on the responsibilities of marriage, children and a family of their own. The sensitive treatment of this theme by Amadi brings out the hopes and aspirations of the young Nigerian girls, and how they are made to feel their responsible role in society.

Amadi's fiction reflects a culture that only fifty years ago was a reality in the whole of West Africa. Some of the very old people living in parts of Nigeria must have a vivid recollection of that old society. When they consider the predicaments of the new order, they must be looking back with nostalgia towards the past, and wondering whether their country has really benefitted from the winds of progress that have changed the face of their land.

NOTES

1. (London: Heinemann Educational Books, 1975).
2. (London: Heinemann Educational Books, 1975).
3. (London: Heinemann Educational Books, 1978).

Fiction across Worlds: Some Writers of Indian Origin in Canada

The Commonwealth is a brotherhood of states spread over all the five continents of the world. The nations that form parts of it have much more in common than only the English language. The Commonwealth countries share areas of creative interest that are often missing in other federations based on common geographical, economic or political considerations. The Canadian nation consists of a multiplicity of races and cultures that is rarely encountered outside the Commonwealth. From time to time, through accidents of history, a variety of people of different races, backgrounds and cultures have sought refuge in this country of the English and French speaking peoples. Multiculturalism is an essential aspect of the Canadian scene, and it is reflected in the works of the writers of this land. It should come as no surprise that their imagination leaps across worlds in search of suitable themes and motifs for creative writing.

There is a great variety in the Canadian immigrant experience as recorded in literature. During the last fifty years, many writers of Indian origin, once or twice removed from their first homeland, have gone as immigrants to Canada. One of the foremost among them was Bharati Mukherjee—now in the USA—who could boast of a triple inheritance from her Bengali Indian antecedents to the years spent in an American university and to the subsequent experience of living and teaching in Canada. In works like *Wife* (1976) and *Jasmine* (1990) she provides a realistic account of the pressures facing an Indian woman in a male-dominated North American society. In collaboration with Clark Blaise, her America-born husband, Bharati Mukherjee wrote a dual autobiography, *Days and Nights in Calcutta* (1977). It is an account of a year they spent together in India. She went to revisit a world she had left, he to explore a world he had married into. The contrast between the two parts of the book stresses the difference in their points of view. Clark Blaise sees the richness of India and the strangeness of his experience. He faithfully records the events of their journey together, as any other foreign tourist would do. Bharati Mukherjee, on the other hand, with her knowledge of Bengali, hears gossip, pain, pressure and privilege of the people she encounters. The same episodes carry different overtones in the two separate accounts. It is the difference between an outsider's and an insider's view. With the publication of the book back in the West, it highlights the contrast between a native and a foreign writer.

The immigrant writer's contribution is best illustrated by a short story, which comes at the end of *The Middleman and Other Stories* (1988), a book of Bharati Mukherjee dealing entirely with the immigrant experience. Entitled "The Management of Grief," it is a fictional account of some Canadians of Indian origin, who have lost their close relatives in the Air India jumbo jet disaster off the coast of Ireland. It is significant that the flight originated in Canada, and was on its way to India. The majority of the travellers were Indians. Being an India-born herself, Bharati Mukherjee expresses the sense of grief of those left behind in Canada more authentically than any native Canadian, American or British writer could. The outlook of one of the characters in the story is pointedly Indian: "Kusum says we can't escape our fate. She says that all those people—our husbands, my boys, her girl with the nightingale voice, all those Hindus, Christians, Sikhs, Muslims, Parsis, and atheists on that plane—were fated to die together off this beautiful bay."[1] Again, note what the narrator, Shaila Bhave, says: "I am trapped between two modes of knowledge. At thirty-six I am too old to start over and too young to give up. Like my husband's spirit, I flutter between worlds." (189)

Another Mukherjee character, Panna Patel, in "A Wife's story" complains, "In my red silk sari I'm conspicuous." (25) This is a conclusion corroborated by Meera Shastri, an Indian immigrant in Canada, in her essay, "Canadian Experience": "Within a week of my arrival in Toronto, I realized that the sari was not a practical outfit for the Canadian winter and took to wearing pants. It was just a short while before I began to feel self-conscious about wearing saris even when the weather was good."[2] Numerous similar observations are reflected in the experiences and writings of Canadian writers of fiction of Indian origin.

Neil Bissoondath, V.S. Naipaul's sister's son, is a West Indian of the East Indian origin. He was born in Trinidad and went in 1973 to Toronto to complete a degree in French at the York University. He stayed on to live and write in Canada. For obvious reasons, his fiction carries the triple flavour of his diverse backgrounds. *Digging up the Mountains* (1985) is a collection of short stories in which he examines the intellectual implications of the motifs of changing places and exchanging cultures. This reminds one of the manner in which Naipaul tackles these themes in some of his early fictional works dealing with the life of the

East Indian immigrants in Trinidad. In one of his essays, Bissoondath refers to the Canadian oil company executive, who was looking for an apartment in Toronto. This man rejected buildings with East Indian tenants because he believed that cockroaches were symbols of good luck in their culture. Such misunderstandings persist and give us some idea of what an author is up against while transforming immigrant experience into fiction.

Nazneen Sadiq was born in Kashmir in 1944. She went to Canada when she was twenty, and stayed on to write fiction that has the flavour of her immigrant experience. Her *Ice Bangles* (1988) is a collection of short stories. In the title story, Naila, the narrator, living in Canada, goes home to attend the wedding of her brother. It comes as a surprise to her that her brother's bride, though quite charming, is dark-skinned. Her comment in this regard is revealing: "The fair-skinned northerners had practised for centuries the same discrimination which their British masters had been accused of. Her mother, who had hoped secretly for a Kashmiri wife for her only son, had been cheated." (*Between Worlds,* 31) When Naila notices the children of the domestic servants peeping over the boundary walls at the glittering festivities, "She was conscious for the first time of social divisions and found them disturbing. Five years of living in Canada had awakened a social conscience which emerged with the embarrassment of adolescent acne." (34)

So far I have referred to three writers of fiction, who coming with their Indian and other backgrounds, write about the immigrant experience in Canada, drawing very much on their first hand experience. They highlight the problems of immigrants confronted with the situation of living in the midst of an alien culture. It creates more problems for them when they go back, even though temporarily, to the places of their birth. Now I would like to draw your attention to a Canadian writer of Indian origin, who, while living in his adopted home, writes most authentically about his experience in India before going to Canada.

Rohinton Mistry, a Parsi, was born in Bombay in 1952, and emigrated to Canada in 1975. For ten years, he worked in a bank, studying English and philosophy part time at the University of Toronto. His first short story fetched him a Hart House Prize for fiction in 1983. His stories have been published in major Canadian literary journals and anthologies. *Such a Long Journey* (1991) is a brilliant first novel by one of the most remarkable writers of fiction to have emerged from India in recent years. It is set in Bombay against the backdrop of the Indo-Pakistan war of 1971 and the emergence of Bangladesh as a separate independent nation. The novel tells the story of a Parsi bank official, Gustad

Noble, and the peculiar way in which the conflict in the Indian sub-continent affects him and his family.

The remarkable thing about *Such a Long Journey* is its absolute Indianness, without any trace of the Canadian immigrant experience that the author must have gone through for fifteen years before the publication of the book. It is steeped in the atmosphere of Bombay, particularly of the exclusive Parsi community of that city. The Khodadad Building, an apartment house, where Gustad Noble lives along with his Parsi neighbours, is a world in itself. Dilnavaz, his wife is beset by the usual Indian superstitions, encouraged by Miss Kutpitia, the mysterious spinster. When Sohrab, the elder son of Gustad, refuses to join the IIT, against the wishes of his father, and leaves home, Dilnavaz circles a lemon over his head, offering the juice of it in a sweetened drink to the half-wit, Tehmul-Lungraa. For general good luck, she hangs a lemon and some green chillies on a string above the front door from inside. Again, she consults Miss Kutpitia, when baffled by the prolonged illness of her daughter, Roshan, in order to devise ways of warding off the evil eye. The world of Indian superstition in *Such a Long Journey* is far removed from the western society of Toronto in Canada, where Rohinton Mistry wrote the novel.

Mistry shows an Indian's knowledge about corruption being an ingrained part of life at all levels in India. He reiterates how an ordinary citizen can get nothing done without bribes, if he has any dealings with the municipality, the police department or the politicians. Dr. Paymaster, the family physician of Gustad Noble, points out: "that municipal corruption was only a microcosmic manifestation of the greed, dishonesty, and moral turpitude that flourished at the country's centre. He described meticulously how, from the very top, whence all power flowed, there also dripped the pus of putrefaction, inflicting every stratum of society below."[3]

Mistry reminds us how goods donated by people to support the war effort at the time of the Chinese invasion later turned up for sale in the Chor Bazaar. He makes critical references to Indira Gandhi's handling of the Bangladesh War. The episode of Nagarwala cheating the State Bank of India of several lakhs of rupees, by impersonating the Prime Minister on the phone, is woven into the fabric of the novel and intermingled with the fate of Major Bilimoria, a friend of Gustad Noble. A notable concern in *Such a Long Journey* is the raw deal that Bilimoria gets from the Government out of working for the RAW. Gustad gets involved in the shady deal and draws his friend, Dinshawji, too into it. The death of Dinshawji from cancer is a high point in the novel, as it reveals the truly noble side of Gustad, who is the sole male mourner at the

Parsi funeral rites that follow. It is a kind of cleansing process that pushes Gustad very close to an intense spiritual experience.

Gustad's dream of launching his son as a successful engineer is a lofty one, and a purely Indian one at that. "The dream of IIT took shape, then took hold of their imaginations. And the Indian Institute of Technology became the promised land. It was El Dorado and Camelot, it was Xanadu and Oz. It was the home of the Holy Grail." (66) One cannot fail to appreciate the tongue-in-the-cheek flavour of this passage.

To his young daughter's question, "Daddy, why is West Pakistan killing the people in East Pakistan?" (81) Gustad can offer only this simplistic answer: "East Pakistan is poor, they said to West, we are always hungry, please give us a fair share. But West said no. Then East said, in that case we don't want to work with you. So, as punishment, West Pakistan is killing and burning East Pakistan." (81) That is as close a summation of the political upheaval as any.

Peerbhoy Paanwala in *Such a Long Journey* is an institution by himself. He has a *paan* for all seasons, but the one most in demand is the bed-breaker or *palungtode paan* with its renowned aphrodisiacal properties. Possessing a rich faculty for myth-making, Peerbhoy suggests that even the Moghul emperors used this variety of *paan* when they went to their harems. To young boys, he would offer a *paan* which would cleanse their heads of boyish impurities and help them concentrate on their studies. When the Bangladesh war is at its apex, Peerbhoy rises to great heights in weaving a myth about the doings of Gen. Yahya Khan and his military governor of East Pakistan.

Gustad Noble's dreams and expectations are modest indeed, but circumstances prevailing in the India of his times conspire to deny him even these. It is very hard on him that he cannot make things happen in such a way as to fulfil his aspirations. Forces, stranger than himself, come in the way of his achieving his ambitions. His elder son does not join the IIT; Roshan, his favourite child, suffers from a prolonged illness; Dinshawji, his best friend, dies of cancer; and another friend, Bilimoria, betrays his trust. Gradually, Gustad Noble modifies his dreams and dilutes his expectations. It is quite obvious that he is not in control of things. But this does not make him turn into a defeatist. In the true oriental way, his triumph consists in the calm manner with which he faces each trial of his life. It lies in his acceptance of the harsh realities of the world to which he belongs. His grandest moment comes towards the end of the novel, when he forgives his erring son, and clasps him to his bosom in a noble gesture of acceptance of Sohrab's decision to lead his own life.

The conclusion that I would like to draw in this brief essay relates to the various ways in which the immigrant writers of Indian origin in Canada convert their experience into fiction. Few among them would opt to project their newly acquired western values, which perhaps they fail to appreciate fully. Some, like Bharati Mukherjee and Nazneen Sadiq, concentrate on the changes in the attitudes and sensibility of their fictional characters, when confronted with the dilemmas of cross-cultural concerns. This is, no doubt, a rewarding way of projecting the Indian immigrant experience in Canada. But we should not under-estimate the contribution of writers of fiction like Rohinton Mistry, who open a window on India for their Canadian and other western readers. *Such a Long Journey* tells us more about the Parsi community in Bombay than a book of sociology possibly could. What is more, Mistry is able to project the emotional life and personal relationships of the Parsis as a valuable part of the wider human experience at the international level by writing about these things from across worlds. The Indian readers of Mistry will react to this book in their own way. For them, he presents an interesting slice of their own life, which for them is a most valued thing. While Salman Rushdie, another Indian expatriate writer, offends with his satiric denunciations, Rohinton Mistry entertains while he exposes the frailties of his characters with his gentle humour and an eye for the comic in human nature.

NOTES

1. Bharati Mukherjee, *The Middleman and Other Stories* (Penguin Books India, 1990), p. 184.
2. Milly Charon, ed., *Between Two Worlds: The Canadian Immigrant Experience* (Montreal: Nu-Age Editions, 1988), p. 284.
3. Rohinton Mistry, *Such a Long Journey* (London: Faber and Faber, 1991), pp. 312-13.

Margaret Laurence's Manawaka in *The Diviners*

In a series of five books, known as the Manawaka novels, Margaret Laurence explores her idea that human societies are built round tribal instincts. These works are *The Stone Angel* (1964), *A Jest of God* (1966), *The Fire-Dwellers* (1969), *A Bird in the House* (1970) and *The Diviners* (1974). The entire sequence concerns the preoccupations of the heroines with their ancestral or ethnic past. All the five protagonists—Hagar Shipley, Rachel Cameron, Stacey MacAindra, Vanessa Macleod and Morag Gunn—are of Scottish origin, living as strangers in a new homeland, the small and remote town called Manawaka. It is, in fact, a transformation of Neepawa in Manitoba, Canada, the birthplace of Margaret Laurence herself. Though the five heroines leave Manawaka at one time or another, they are not able to dissociate themselves from it emotionally. Following the example of her creator, Morag Gunn of *The Diviners* goes on a kind of pilgrimage to discover her roots in Scotland. But she returns disillusioned to Canada, realizing that her real home is in the new land, that her ethnic identity belongs to the provincial town of Manawaka. While narrating the story of her heroine, from infancy to middle-aged motherhood, from an early hesitant schoolgirl short story writer to an established and recognized novelist, Margaret Laurence also develops the theme of the provincial Scottish society of Manawaka. This paper is an attempt at examining how successful she is in projecting her ethnic concerns.

William Faulkner created Yoknapatawpha as the geographical location of his fiction, and R.K. Narayan transformed Mysore into the Malgudi of his stories and novels. In the same tradition Margaret Laurence presents Manawaka, a small Canadian prairie town, harbouring a community of the descendants of the Scottish settlers. The presence of the town is sensitively evoked through extended flashbacks in *The Diviners*. Though Manawaka does not exist on a map, the significant point is that Laurence is able to use the fictitious town and its environs as a locale for five of her works of fiction. The place-name has a Canadian-Indian suggestion like that of Neepawa, which is its original. The same is true of the River Wachakawa that winds through the ups and downs of the slopes and valleys on the periphery of Manawaka. The town boasts of a few well-stocked stores on Main Street, a bakery, two cafes (Parthenon and Regal), an elementary and two high schools (the Manawaka Collegiate and the Public School), some farms spread around the hill-sides, and, the last but not the least, a dump which is known as the Nuisance Grounds in the local parlance.

Morag Gunn, the heroine of *The Diviners*, is an orphan girl, who lives with her foster-parents, Christie Logan and Prin (short for Princess), in a ramshackle house on Hill Street, which links up with Main Street. The Manawaka community is small enough for everybody to know everybody else. They are familiar with the names of each other's distant relations, and are fully aware of what is going on behind each closed door. It is a well-knit society where petty jealousies are rampant, but where again the bond of neighbourhood prompts one to come to the rescue of another at all times. What would be the fate of a five year old orphan like Morag Gunn, when both her parents die together, in a big city like Toronto, can be anybody's guess. But at Manawaka kindly neighbours look after her, and provide her with foster-parents and a home. When the casualty lists of the Battle of Dieppe reach Manawaka, it becomes an occasion for communal mourning: "There are many dead who will not be buried in the Manawaka cemetery upon the hill where the tall spruces stand like dark angels. There are a great many families who now have fewer sons, or none."[1] They rally round like the branches of a clan, and share the common grief.

Some of the characters that figure in the other Manawaka novels, like Vanessa Macleod and Stacey Cameron, also put in an appearance in *The Diviners*, without having a major role in the action of the novel. Most of the people bear Scottish names, such as, Duncan, Doherty, McCann, Macdonald, Macalister, McKee, Maclaren, Maclachlan, MacIntosh, MacMurtie, Macpherson and McVitie. The only divergent element in this Canadian Scottish society is a family of the Métis or French-Indian half-breeds, the Tonnerres of the Galloping Mountain, occupying a few shacks down the valley on the outskirts of the town. They form a distinct ethnic group by themselves, having little in common with the descendants of the Scottish settlers. The only thing they share is Manawaka, a remote corner of Canada, that vast country of a great variety of ethnic groups.

The central human relationship in *The Diviners* is that of Morag Gunn and her lover, Jules Tonnerre, who fathers her daughter Pique (short for Piquette). Morag is a descendant of the Gunns who migrated long ago from Sutherland, and Jules is a Métis, whose father, Lazarus, comes from the Galloping Mountain. They get to know each other at the Manawaka school, and remain life-long friends and occasional lovers. Morag and Jules together provide the main romantic and human interest in *The Diviners.* But Margaret Laurence also introduces through them her concern with national identity and ethnic past. William H. New includes Laurence among those Canadian writers who find it difficult to avoid such preoccupations. He writes in this context: "Searching for the national identity is a kind of congenital art form in Canada which has provided both the theme for many poets and novelists and the substance of much critical observation and expectation."[2] New is not very much taken up by the recurrence of works of this kind in Canadian literature. It would appear as if for a writer to have the urge to explore his ethnic past is a kind of 'congenital disease.' New is also bothered by the multiculturalism, which exerts its own influence on the way the Canadians assert their identity. But then, one is not always bound to agree with him on this or other issues. The success with which Margaret Laurence projects the theme of ethnic identity, through both Morag and Jules, more than refutes the objections of New.

It is true that Morag and Jules of Manawaka are inheritors of two different strains of national identity, the Scottish-Canadian and the French-Indian. Yet they never have any objections to their common Canadian nationality. What is more, they share an interest in each other's ancestry and traditions. Christie Logan infects Morag with his fascination for the Old Country, Sutherland in Scotland. As a child, she listens to his fervent accounts of the exploits of Piper Gunn, who came with his wife, another Morag, leading his people to the new land. In Christie's words, "he was a great tall man, a man with the voice of drums and the heart of a child and the call of a thousand and the strength of conviction. . . . When Piper Gunn played, the very seagulls echoed the chants of mourning, and the people wept." (49-50) Piper Gunn came piping across the Atlantic, over the prairies and down the Red River to some place in the neighbourhood of Manawaka, and settled there. Morag knows what Christie tells her is part history and part myth, but she listens avidly, and treasures the memory.

A similar kind of experience is repeated by Jules Tonnerre, whose father tells him about Rider Tonnerre, the legendary Métis horseman, who led the resistance of his tribe against the British colonizers. In the tradition of King Arthur receiving the gift of his sword Excalibur from the Lady of the Lake, Rider Tonnerre dreams of a white horse and gets it too after spending a whole night near a haunted lake. The horse is known as *Roi du lac*, King of the Lake, and fetches its master his celebrated title. Here, Margaret Laurence is obviously drawing a parallel between the ancestor of Morag and that of Jules. One is a Gunn, with his reputation for playing pipes, and the other is a Tonnerre, famous for his skill in handling horses. Morag, a mid-twentieth century educated Canadian girl, is the enchanted listener of both the accounts, receiving one from Christie Logan and the other from Jules. The two legends meet in Jules's narration of the Métis rebellion against the British in the nineteenth century, which is the same as Christie's Tale of Piper Gunn and the Rebels. Morag, in a way, symbolizes the modern Canadian inheritor of the multiple cultures of her past. Pique, her daughter, combines in her veins the blood of three races—French, Indian and Scottish. The three ethnic groups unite to form one common Canadian identity in the provincial society of Manawaka. While Morag preserves the tradition by writing stories and novels based on it, Jules perpetuates it by composing and singing songs in celebration of the Tonnerre clan. Even W.H. New admits that Canadian writers 'evoke the many different voices and viewpoints that make up the national pattern.'[3] Margaret Laurence is part of this tradition.

Through a skilful use of the flashback technique in *The Diviners*—'Memorybank Movie,' 'Snapshot' and 'Innerfilm'—Margaret Laurence builds the provincial society of an exclusive ethnic group at Manawaka. They are all mostly of Scottish descent, with traditions, conventions, habits and interests that throw back to the time when their ancestors came from Scotland and settled in the vicinity of Manawaka. The flashbacks build a bridge with the past, and the history of the migrations of the ethnic group falls into its proper perspective. There are numerous references to the Gaelic tradition. On one occasion, Christie recites to Morag a powerful poem of Ossian, rendered into modern English by Macpherson, and later both of them try to read the poem in its original Gaelic version. The whole exercise is very interesting, and links up the present situation of the Scottish ethnic society in Canada with its past cultural tradition. That clearly shows how involved Margaret Laurence is in preserving and projecting the ethnic values of the provincial society of Manawaka, which is after all a small but precious portion of Canada.

The story of the Métis family, which Laurence introduces by way of a complementary contrast to the main plot, only highlights the preoccupations of the main ethnic community of the prairie town. The physical and emotional attraction that Morag Gunn and Jules Tonnerre feel for each other throws up a complication that remains the centre of interest in the novel. Incidentally, in the footsteps of Margaret Laurence herself, Morag feels compelled to leave the town in order to achieve her ambition of becoming a creative writer. Her strong urge to get away from the stifling and confining atmosphere of Manawaka is not to be interpreted as an individual's attempt to dissociate herself from the society to which she belongs, but as her aspiration to secure an independent foothold in the world. To attain this end, Morag takes on the whole world ranged against her, and succeeds in holding her head high in spite of all the odds. But her perseverance, struggle and ultimate achievement should not blind us to the fact of her aspiration of discovering her ethnic roots in Scotland. Even after the birth of her daughter, Pique, she goes on a pilgrimage of discovery to England. At that time she is still trying to find her feet as a writer. A chance meeting with Dan McRaith, a Scottish painter, takes her to Crombruach, a fishing village, wherefrom she could easily go to Sutherland. But at the very last moment, she declines to accept the offer of her guide to take her there, as she realizes that her true identity is inseparable from Manawaka, 'Christie's real country. Where I was born!' (390) The truth discovered by Morag is equally applicable to all others belonging to Manawaka.

In the process of telling the story of the struggles and success of Morag Gunn, a Manawakan orphan, Margaret Laurence also projects the trials and tribulations, the joys and sorrows, the comedy and tragedy of the colonial Scottish community that finds transplanted roots in a new country, Canada. The fact of *The Diviners* becoming a number one best-seller in the very year of its publication is an indication that Laurence did not fail in her object of projecting the need of realizing one's ethnic identity. She is not just an ethnic Canadian writer in a provincial society, but one who speaks for her nation and country.

NOTES

1. Margaret Laurence, *The Diviners* (Toronto: Bantam Books, 1975), p. 143.
2. W.H. New, *Among Worlds* (Erin, Ontario: Press Porcepic, 1975), p. 101.
3. W.H. New, p. 102.

One Woman against the World: Morag Gunn in Margaret Laurence's *The Diviners*

Reviewing the work of Margaret Laurence from 1960, when she published her first novel, to the end of her writing days, one tends to agree with W.J. Keith, in whose view 'Laurence occupies a crucial transitional position in Canadian literature.'[1] Other novelists have written epics about the Indian and Métis rebellions of the nineteenth century, but Laurence and Alice Munro have reconstructed the more recent past of their own childhood and early youth. Margaret Laurence discovered her urge to write while she was outside Canada. Travels with her engineer husband, Jack Laurence, took her to several under-developed African countries, such as Somaliland and the Gold Coast (before it was renamed as Ghana). Her first two books, a novel called *This Side Jordan* (1960) and a collection of short stories entitled *The Tomorrow Tamer* (1963), are both set in the Gold Coast. The African experience gave her a feeling that human societies were built round tribal instincts. She observed and studied the working of these instincts in family, class, ethnic group and nation.

In the five Manawaka works of fiction—*The Stone Angel*, *A Jest of God*, *The Fire-Dwellers*, *A Bird in the House* (a collection of short stories) and *The Diviners*—Margaret Laurence explores her sense of human tribalism. Besides expressing a peculiarly Canadian sensibility, she generally presents women's attitudes. The basic problem of every individual, man or woman, in the modern world is one of survival. This is the major concern of Laurence in the Manawaka series of fiction. What she is vitally interested in projecting is the feminine point of view of life in the mid-twentieth century. In the process, she displays the broad spectrum of the Canadian experience of that time. This essay is an attempt at analyzing the struggle and achievement of a representative Laurence heroine, Morag Gunn of *The Diviners*.

The Diviners is the fifth and last of the Manawaka series. It is a sensitively written account of a helpless, orphan girl, from infancy—through childhood, adolescence and youth—to independent womanhood. While narrating the story of the development of Morag

Gunn, Margaret Laurence also records the process of her rise from a hesitant and shy short story writer to a successful and famous novelist. Every reader of *The Diviners* is bound to ask himself (or herself), which story is the more significant, whether of the woman seeking independence, or of the writer desiring self-expression. The two careers, like the two ambitions, run parallel to each other. Laurence employs the double-narrative technique of two time-spans in developing her theme. The novel is divided into five sections—'River of Now and Then,' 'The Nuisance Grounds,' 'Halls of Sion,' 'Rites of Passage,' and 'The Diviners.' There are nine chapters in all, each beginning with a short account of the present, where Morag is already an established novelist, going through the trials, of raising a teen-aged daughter, Pique, and writing her books at the same time. But the main, powerful and fascinating story of the struggles of an independent woman and her urgent need for love is told through extended flashbacks, which Laurence calls Memorybank Movie. Other devices of shorter pieces, Snapshot and Innerfilm, are also used to supplement the flashbacks, wherever necessary.

After losing both her parents, victims of infantile paralysis, Morag Gunn is brought up by a childless couple of Manawaka—Christie Logan and his wife Prin. Christie is the town scavenger, who collects and carries rubbish to the dumping ground, known as the Nuisance Grounds. This creates problems for Morag, when she goes to school, where the other children taunt her with the profession of her foster-father. Inwardly, she suffers much, but bravely does not let on. Early in life she learns the wisdom of not arguing with adults. This is the way for her to survive. When a kindly neighbour explains to the five- year-old orphan that she has to go and live with the Logans, "Morag says nothing. She has learned you can't argue when you are a kid. You can only wait not to be a kid any more."[2]

Another lesson that she learns early is 'never let them know you are scared.' (34) Growing up at Manawaka is for Morag a toughening process. She feels alienated from the town society, as the only way to survive is by putting distance between herself and a world that does not seem to want her. During these years of crisis, what sustains Morag is her individual fighting spirit and the father's love she gets from Christie. He fires her young impressionable imagination with tales of her Scottish ancestor, Piper Gunn, who came piping all the way from Sutherland, over the Atlantic, across the prairies, putting heart into his people, till he brought them to the farmlands on the banks of the Red River. However, to seek social and economic freedom, Morag resolves to leave Manawaka. The idea of putting a great distance between herself and the shabby town attracts her like a beacon shining from afar. "Now she knows one thing for sure. Nothing—*nothing*—is going to endanger her chances of getting out of Manawaka. And on her own terms, not the town's." (153) But when the time, finally, comes for Morag to depart from Manawaka to seek higher education at Winnipeg, her feeling of jubilation is mixed with that of guilt at being so eager to run away from the place of her birth.

As already pointed out, it is a moot point whether the leading concern of Margaret Laurence in *The Diviners* is to write the success story of a novelist coming, like herself, from the backwoods of Canada, or to demonstrate the strength and fortitude of a woman, who learns to live and love exactly the way she wants, and who is prepared to take on the whole world for the sake of her independence. Apparently, the growth of the woman overshadows the other development, which is subservient to the main issue. Laurence depicts phases in the growth of the woman—child, girl, young woman, wife, and middle-aged mother. The child Morag grows into a young girl, whose need for love is both physical as well as emotional. Jules Tonnerre, a Métis (French-Indian halfbreed) school fellow of Morag, adds to her experience by initiating her in the mystery of sex.

Many years later, Jules turns up again in Morag's life, when she is trying hard to make a success of her marriage with Brooke Skelton, a university professor at Toronto. The husband refuses to let her become a mother. While the woman in Morag clamours for fulfilment by having a child of her own, the self-centred Brooke keeps postponing the event for one reason or another. On an impulse, Morag leaves home to find temporary shelter with Jules. She conceives after reunion with her former lover, who is of too individualistic a spirit to be tied down to marriage and family, but he does not mind if the woman wants a child from him. It is highly ironic that the two men with whom Morag gets passionately involved follow their own dreams, without really caring for her feelings. This, in fact, move her feminine sensibility to work for independence and attainment, away from the world of men. Laurence suggests that woman's dependence on man is not so much an emotional, as a biological necessity, which becomes a cause of unnecessary mental torture for the heroine of *The Diviners*. Brooke does not bring credit to himself by refusing to comply with the wishes of his wife, who is just a plaything to him, without an independent entity. He is too much involved in furthering his own professional status to care for Morag's intense craving for motherhood. Her femininity feels outraged. She breaks up the marriage in order to exercise her freedom to have a child. Conceiving out of wedlock does not bother her in the least. Morag is bold and defiant in her disregard of social taboos. What matters, in the end, is that she gets what she wants. Divorced from Brooke, she gives birth to a daughter, who she names after Piquette, the dead sister of Jules Tonnerre.

Christie and his tales of Piper Gunn give Morag an abiding interest in her ancestral past. Struggling to establish herself as a writer, she journeys to London, where she finds work as a book-seller's assistant. She meets a Scottish painter named McRaith, and they become friends. He offers to take Morag and Pique to Sutherland, the region in Scotland to which the Gunns originally belonged. For Morag, it is a kind of pilgrimage to discover her ancestral roots. They first go to McRaith's home at Crombruach, a small fishing village. But when he wants to drive her to Sutherland, Morag unexpectedly turns down his offer. Obviously, her thinking is changed after reaching Scotland. She tells McRaith:

> 'I don't know that I can explain. It has to do with Christie. The myths are my reality. . . . I don't need to go there because I know now what it was I had to learn here. . . . I always thought it was the land of my ancestors, but is not.'
>
> 'What is then?'
>
> 'Christie's real country. Where I was born.' (390)

Soon after this episode, Morag rushes back to Canada to visit Christie on his death-bed at Manawaka. Later she buys a farm-house at Maconnell's Landing, on the banks of a river. For the first time in her life, she writes her novels in tranquillity of mind and natural surroundings. At the end of her struggle and wanderings, she feels at home with her neighbours, the river and the changing seasons. The passage of time is marked by the movements of the migratory birds, the swallows and Canadian geese. Like them, Pique too has a life of her own. She keeps going off on her jaunts in different directions. Morag worries about her daughter, but dares not interfere directly in her life. The mother has lived an independent life, and naturally hesitates to try shaping the destiny of the daughter.

The final image of *The Diviners* is of Morag living her solitary life at Maconnell's Landing, devoting herself whole-heartedly to writing, the dominant passion of her life. The reference to a nineteenth century work, *The Canadian Settler's Guide* (1855), indicates her interest in history as well as feeling for women writers. She reflects appreciatively on the achievement of her predecessor: "Catherine Parr Traill, mid-1800s, botanist, drawing and naming wildflowers, writing a guide for settlers with one hand, whilst rearing a brace of young and working like a galley slave with the other." (95) Morag feels so much involved with C.P.

Traill that she is frequently in the habit of carrying on imaginary conversations with that worldly wise woman. This serves her instead of the feminine companionship, which she misses in her lonely existence, especially when Pique is away from home.

Royland, a neighbour who makes his living by divining wells for the farmers in the surrounding country, suddenly loses his miraculous gift. Morag retains her own skill of creative writing. But she is not quite sure how effective her novels are, how useful to the readers. Margaret Laurence comments: "At the least Royland knew he had been a true diviner. There were the wells, proof positive. . . . Morag's magic tricks were of a different order. She would never know whether they actually worked or not, or to what extent." (452)

Still, Morag Gunn has a sense of achievement at having surmounted all odds and become one of the literary diviners of the world. Eventually, she has established her identity as a woman by succeeding in her chosen field against stiff opposition.

NOTES

1. W.J. Keith, *Canadian Literature in English* (New York: Longman, 1985), p. 160.
2. Margaret Laurence, *The Diviners* (Toronto: Bantam Books, 1975), p. 17.

Feminism and Femininity in a Colonial Context: Margaret Atwood's *Surfacing* and Margaret Laurence's *The Diviners*

Even a superficial survey of the twentieth century Canadian literature shows that there has been an upsurge of feminism in it during the past thirty years. In the sixties and seventies, the rise of and success achieved by such women writers of merit as Margaret Laurence (1926-1987), Alice Munro (b. 1931) and Margaret Atwood (b. 1939) is something truly remarkable. Laurence's chief concern as a novelist is the portrayal of character. A powerfully realized woman is at the centre of each of her novels, for example, Hagar Shipley in *The Stone Angel* (1964), Rachel Cameron in *A Jest of God* (1966), Stacey MacAindra in *The Fire Dwellers* (1969), and Morag Gunn in *The Diviners* (1974). By contrast, Munro excels at revealing the surprising depth and complexity in the emotional life of simple, ordinary people. As Joan Coldwell writes, "Such revelations are often filtered through the consciousness of a girl who feels herself to be 'different' from those around her, usually because she is a secretly developing artist in an environment alien and hostile to art."[1]

Lives of Girls and Women (1971) foresees a time when women will not assess their worth only through their relationship with men. But *Who do you think you are?* (1978) shows how different it is for even the most competent women to break the vital 'connection.' In each of the novels of Margaret Atwood, the main character is again a woman living a professional life in a modern consumer society. Her protagonists are forced to engage in a radical process of reassessment when the props supporting their carefully constructed version of themselves are knocked out from under them. This is seen as much in *The Edible Woman* (1969), *Lady Oracle* and *The Handmaid's* Tale (1985), as in *Surfacing* (1972), the novel I am concentrating on in this essay.

The three Canadian writers mentioned above have one thing in common, which is their feminism. But I would like to distinguish between two divergent attitudes of the female mind, feminism and femininity. For this purpose, I have chosen one text each of Margaret

Atwood and Margaret Laurence, *Surfacing* and *The Diviners*, to make a point of distinction between the two notable feminist writers. The recent development of feminism in post-colonial Canadian literature is, in fact, part of a wider global feminist movement. Among other fields, it expresses itself in such diverse human activities as sports and academics. Women are no longer hesitant to assert their identity as something independent of and separate from men. The establishment of special chairs for women's studies at institutions of higher learning has already attained world-wide recognition.

Feminism is defined as a bold criticism of the prevailing social conditions, which have excluded women from the dominant male culture, social, sexual, political and intellectual pursuits. The feminist theory rose to prominence in the 1980s within the Women's Lib Movement. The strategies of the feminist theory are largely focused on politics, sexual oppression, patriarchal prejudice, wage inequalities, discriminatory employing practices, and women's universal invisibility within a male-dominated culture. The feminist writings of 1970s and 1980s have the raising of women's (and subsequently society's) consciousness as central to the social and political movement. A convergence of female social activists, theorists, artists, writers, historians and critics evolved, whose aim was to understand modes of perception, psychological factors, and patterns of thought peculiar to the sex. Such male terms of endearment for women as the better half, fair sex, gentle sex, etc., are denounced by the torch-bearers of feminism. In their eyes, woman is not only equal but superior to man. Revolting against the Freudian theories of sexuality which emphasize male development, the feminist writers reject traditions of western psychiatry, and elevate woman from a subordinate, derivative—the proverbial biblical left rib of Adam—and apolitical position in the family unit, in particular, and in society, in general. The fictional works of both Margaret Laurence and Margaret Atwood are significant contributions to the world-wide feminist movement.

Canada was the first British Colony to attain dominion status in 1867, when the Victorian Empire was at its height. However, even now, after nearly one hundred and fifty years, the British Sovereign appoints the Governor General of Canada. During the second half of the last century, Canadian literature began its wandering course primarily on a nationalistic note. But it took all of one hundred years for this literature to establish itself and branch off into new channels. The feminist literature of the present century is a by-product of the new cross-currents. The Canadian feminist literature is characterized by an urge to vindicate the social and political status of women, while asserting the nationalistic aspirations at the same time. Margaret Atwood's *Surfacing* is a feminist novel, which also projects the Canadian identity under threat from politically and economically powerful Americanism. The warning is sounded in the very opening sentence of the novel: "I can't believe I'm on this road again, twisting along past the lake where the white birches are dying, the disease is spreading up from the south, and I notice they now have sea-planes for hire."[2] The Americans too came across from the south.

According to George Woodcock, the literary critic, Atwood suggests in *Survival*, a reflective prose work which appeared in 1972, the same year as *Surfacing*, that it is the colonial situation that has made Canadian writing a literature of failure. It presents an attitude to life that aims no higher than survival. She isolates a familiar Christian syndrome: in Canada, they have no heroes, only martyrs. All Canadian attitudes are related to the central fact of victimization. Survival without triumph is the only way out of the failure that is the characteristic theme of a high proportion of Canadian writing. *Surfacing* is a novel that is mainly concerned with survival. Its unnamed narrator and protagonist explores her own past. A migrant into a new self, the martyred heroine herself breaks the jail of her imprisoned spirit. Canada is projected as the victim of a sickness of colonialism. The heroine, whose death is a high point in the action of the novel, is wantonly killed not by Americans, but by Canadians who are no different from Americans. *Surfacing* is a novel of self-realization that includes an element of self-criticism. For the young narrator, it is a journey into her past, which is really a journey into her feminine self. The events unfolding out of a return to the scene of her childhood enable her to realize herself as a whole being. In this retreat into the wilderness, Atwood challenges the western ways of looking at things, particularly of relating to nature. She presents a primitive and mystical participation in nature, through which the heroine virtually recreates herself.

In *Surfacing*, Atwood projects a rebellious feministic approach to life's experience of a young woman with an artistic bent of mind. She has been estranged from her parents for nine years, during which she gets married, bears a son, but now lives separately from her husband, who has the custody of the child. Early on in the novel, she says of her son, "But I couldn't have brought the child here, I never identified it as mine; I didn't name it before it was born even, the way you are supposed to. It was my husband's, he imposed it on me, all the time it was growing in me I felt like an incubator." (37)

The narrative reflects the tortured sensibility of a woman who is not prepared to compromise with the male-dominated society, and is looking for routes of escape. The news of the mysterious disappearance of her botanist father, from his cabin on a lake island, gives her an excuse for revisiting the environ that surrounded her early years. The journey of discovery and exploration along with her three companions—Joe, her lover, and a couple named David and Anna—is a virtual spiritual quest, which ends in a nerve-shattering climax. The narrator tolerates her lover only as a sexual partner, without submitting to his male superiority. Rummaging through the book-shelves of her father, she comes across some books of 'the eighteenth century rationalists,' whom he admired and recommended for her study when she was a young girl. But later, her husband had revealed to her that "Burns was an alcoholic, Cowper was a madman, Doctor Johnson a manic-depressive and Goldmith a pauper. There was something wrong with Thompson also; . . . After that I liked them better, they weren't paragons any more." (42) It is a significant comment that the narrator makes when she says no man has made her sad since her husband: 'A Divorce is like an amputation, you survive but there's less of you.' (46) Such a revealing statement could come only from a zealous feminist like Margaret Atwood.

The anonymous heroine of *Surfacing* presents through her narrative involving two time spans—past childhood juxtaposed with present adulthood—the eternal dilemma of man-woman relationship. The question is one of dominance, which is perhaps, the basic issue underlying all feminist literature. Atwood's protagonist expresses her intolerance of enslaving marital ties, even denial of the on-going physical relationship with Joe. The reader is constantly reminded of the superficiality of the ideas and endeavours of males like David, Joe and the American tourists with their sleek and swift powerboats. The feminist narrator seems more tolerant of the earthy Anna, just because she is another woman. Yet her over-dependence on make-up, which is always 'slabbed down on her face like a vision,' (176) is continuously brought up disparagingly. Anna is described in feminist terms as "a seamed and folded imitation of a magazine picture that is itself an imitation of a woman who is also an imitation, the original nowhere." (177)

On the island, it is the heroine of *Surfacing* who is in control of things—showing the men where and how to fish, teaching them the fundamentals of canoeing, cleaning and cooking the food with some help from Anna, leading the group through secret pathways into the mysterious places deep in the woods. As the narrative proceeds, she gradually withdraws herself from the male-dominated society. Eventually, she rejects human ties, seeking a return to primitivism, rather stark animalism, closest to the state of nature. Her feminist instinct prompts her to trick Joe into unwillingly helping her in conceiving another child, with the sole aim of bringing it up on birth in the lap of nature, away from the taint of human civilization.

In contrast to the rebellious feminism of Atwood's *Surfacing*, Margaret Laurence presents in her Manawaka series of fiction a balanced attitude towards feminism and femininity. This is best illustrated by reference to her last novel, *The Diviners*. The childhood experience and dilemma of Morag Gunn are no less complex and bewildering than those of the drifting heroine of *Surfacing*. Seeking her own individual identity and recognition as a writer, Morag leaves the confining and suffocating society of Manawaka to achieve the flowering of her intellect and creative sensibility at Winnipeg. Later, when she reflects on the plight of the pioneering colonical women of Canada, she makes the following conclusions: "Women working like horses. Also probably pregnant most of time. Baking bread in brick ovens, with a loaf in their own ovens. Looking after broods of chickens and kids. Terrible. Appalling."[3]

But, before this realization, she has to go through the pains of growing up, both as an adopted orphan girl and as a budding writer. At high school, the Manawaka Collegiate, she feels a prisoner in the narrow world of the small Canadian prairie town. However, she reflects: "But if you work, really work, and get educated, something will come of it, maybe. Like being able to get out of Manawaka and never come back. Morag listens at nights to the long waiting of the trains. . . . One day she will be on one of those trains, going to the city and maybe even further than the city. Going to the whole world." (120-21) In this childish but deeply sensitive reflection one notices that young Morag has the makings of an ardent feminist. At the college in Winnipeg, Morag poses a puzzling question to her teacher of English literature, Brooke Skelton:

> "What I can't understand about Donne, though, is . . . how is it he can know so much about people's feelings and then write so many cruel lines?"
>
> "Which cruel lines did you have in mind?" Dr. Skelton enquires, looking surprised. . . . "Well, like 'For God's sake hold your tongue and let me love.' That's a very cruel line. Supposing the lady had been able to write poetry—I mean, you wonder what she might have said to *him*." (191)

Morag's teacher is so astounded at this ingenious comment that he gradually feels drawn towards her, and, some years later, they marry and settle down at Toronto. But after her marriage she becomes a victim of a male chauvinism of Brooke Skelton, who concentrates on his academic career, suppressing Morag's desire to have a child. In desperation, she takes the initiative in breaking up the marriage, a bold act that confirms her feminist outlook. Yet she reveals an unmistakable streak of feminity in romantically turning to the Metis singer, Jules Tonnerre, who was her first lover at Manawaka. Morag conceives his child out of wedlock, and feels fulfilled as a woman only after giving birth to a daughter, whom she names Piqutte after the dead sister of Jules. For a single woman, living by herself, this is as bold a step as her earlier decision to leave Manawaka in her quest of success as a writer. If the first action is motivated by the fierce enthusiasm of a feminist in the making, the later enterprise comes about only due to her natural feminine yearning for motherhood. By a symbolic coincidence, Morag's daughter and her first published novel appear more or less together. Other literary successes follow to make easy the daunting task of looking after a growing daughter in a challenging world.

Atwood's nameless protagonist in *Surfacing* is a hard-boiled feminist, who thinks nothing of separating from a husband and son that shackle her freedom and individuality. Later, she suppresses her feminity by turning down the marital proposal of Joe who loves her, but whom she does not love in return, only tolerates as a physical necessity. In the end, she rejects human society and turns to primitive animalism. In *The Diviners*, Laurence's Morag Gunn of Scotttish extraction faces the dilemma of trying to live her own life as a writer, while coping with the emotional and physical demands of being wife and mother, by turns. Her liaison with the Metis youth, Jules Tonnerre, produces a daughter whose consciousness of her mixed heritage, painful though it is, holds the promise of a better future. At the end of novel, Morag is a successfully established novelist, one of the diviners of the world, who asserts her femininity with the caring heart of a mother. Apprehension for how the readers receive her books is more than matched by her affection and concern for Pique. The obvious conclusions to be derived from the comparison attempted here hardly need a reiteration at the end of this essay.

NOTES

1. Entry on Alice Munro, *The Oxford Companion to Canadian Literature*, ed. William Toye (Toronto: 0UP, 1983), p. 537.
2. Margaret Atwood, *Surfacing* (Markham, Ontario: Paperbacks, 1973), p. 7.
3. Margaret Laurence, *The Diviners* (Toronto: McClelland and Steward-Bantam , 1975), p. 94.

An East-African Indian Fictional Cocktail from Canada: M.G. Vassanji's *The Gunny Sack*

The three quotes, taken from three different sources, that follow, focus attention on the immigrant experience in Africa and Canada, which is the central theme of *The Gunny Sack*, the award-winning first novel of M.G. Vassanji, the Toronto-based East-African writer of Indian extraction. Published in 1989, it was followed by another novel, *No New Land* (1991) and a collection of short stories, *Uhuru Street* (1992). A third novel, *The Book of Secrets*, appeared in 1994.

The first passage, to which I would like to draw attention is from 'Sojourners,' an essay by the American writer, Annie Dillard: "I alternate between thinking of the planet as home . . . and as a hard land of exile in which we are all sojourners. . . . We don't know where we belong, . . . Our life seems cursed to be . . . a wandering without end."[1] And, then, there is the Japanese poet, Takeo Nakano, who says in a poem entitled 'My Hands,'

> My hands tremble
> As I sign my naturalization papers
> Making me a Canadian citizen
> And Canada my final resting place.[2]

Lastly, here is what Darius Cooper, the India-born poet living at San Diego in the USA, writes in a poem called 'What is India to Me as Now in my Extinguished Immortality I Scream':

> It is the crack in the pavement
> where I had once buried the dream
> of secretly, one day, going away . . .
>
> I had thought
> that journeys to a foreign land
> would make my stagnant soul
> acquire fresh metaphors.

I was wrong my friends,
I was wrong.
Do not envy me.
Do not envy me
as now in my extinguished immortality
I scream
What is India to me.[3]

My submission is that these three significant passages hint at the existence of a growing genre of writing in Canada, England, and America, the immigrant literature of a mixed inheritance, to which belongs *The Gunny Sack* of M.G. Vassanji.

Today, the entire scenario of fictional writing all over the world presents a vastly different picture from what it was in the nineteenth century. The gradual break up of the former British empire is a major factor behind this global phenomenon. The other reason is the jet-age revolution in international transport, which facilitates migrations of communities across the continents, leading to the establishing of multicultural societies in different parts of the world. In Canada, writers of multiple races, hues, cultures and backgrounds flourish together to produce a kaleidoscopic variety of literature. The authors of South Asian origin, however remote their antecedents and links with the land of their ancestors, have made substantial contributions to the richness of Canadian fiction. In this context, the names that readily come to mind are those of Bharati Mukherjee, Adil Jussawala, Ondaatje, Zulfikar Ghose, Neil Bissoondath, Rohinton Mistry and M.G. Vassanji.

The appearance of Vassanji on the Canadian scene as a writer of fiction, and his great popularity across the Commonwealth countries are linked with the modern phenomenon of immigrant literature. He was born in Kenya, went to school in Tanzania, and received his higher education in the USA. Now, he lives in Toronto, Canada, where he writes, and edits *The Toronto Review*. Such diversity of background equips him well to emerge as a novelist of ample promise from among the immigrant Canadian writers. *The Gunny Sack*, as the very title suggests, is a delightful pot pourri of several narratives and characters of mixed antecedents. Salim Juma, the Tanzanian Asian protagonist, is the great grandson of an African woman slave, but he also retains cultural and linguistic links with his Gujarati Indian heritage. The novel is the repository of the collective consciousness of several Asian Africans such as Dhanji Govindji, Ji Bai, Kulsum and others. It has been described as Africa's (and Canada's) answer to Salman Rushdie's *Midnight's Children*, the central figure of which is, incidentally, named Saleem

Sinai. In this essay an attempt is made to place *The Gunny Sack* of Vassanji, a joint product of Indian, African and Canadian experience, in the context of the changing global scenario in the second half of the twentieth century.

Even before the reader starts on his journey of discovery of this sea of a novel, he notices several interesting things about it, which provoke his thought. First, the author of *The Gunny Sack* acknowledges his thanks to the Ontario Arts Council and Multiculturalism Directorate (Canada) for assistance in publishing the novel. Secondly, the non-English words, mostly in Swahili and Cutchi-Gujarati, are intended to be integral to the text. Thirdly, it is a work of fiction, with some historical events and characters serving as background. Fourthly, the keynote of the novel is struck by W.B. Yeats's line from 'Vacillation': 'Let all things pass away.' The choice of the word 'sea' to describe the novel is deliberate. For, even as it maintains the tradition of the European realistic novel in its selective combination of fact and fiction, *The Gunny Sack* also relates to the Indian epic tradition of the *Mahabharata* and the *Kathasaritsagar*, the latter literally meaning a sea of fiction formed by the mingling of several streams of narrative. Vassanji's novel conforms to that description as it mingles the Indian-Gujarati strains with the Zanzibari-Kenyan-Tanzanian elements of African origin. And, then, this heady cocktail was mixed in Toronto, a major centre of immigrant cultures in Canada. The linguistic features of the novel—European, African and Asian—are part of its exquisite flavour, and do full justice to the multicultural fare served by the author. *The Gunny Sack* offers such a skilful blend of tragedy and comedy, *viraha* (separation) and union, that one keeps wondering what to expect next even to the end. The reader could not ask for a better suggestive introductory line than the wise saying of Yeats: 'Let all things pass away.'

There is so much happening all the time in *The Gunny Sack*—good and bad, joyous and sad—that one has only to wait for the narrative to come to its logical end in order to enjoy its full flavour. The novel emerges out of the collective memory of a small overseas East-African community in Canada, the Shamsis, originally the Gujarati followers of Shamas Pir, who, long ago, promised his disciples a saviour from the west. "Now it seemed to some that he had come, not a pir, but a Pierre, Trudeau of Canada, promising a cold El dorado in the north. He will take us, they said, as he took the Ugandans, leave it to Pierre True-do!"[4]

The collective memory of the central Shamsi family in the novel is held together by Ji Bai, who comes as a teen-ager from a remote village in Gujarat to become the matriarch of a wide-spread clan in East-Africa. 'Memory, Ji Bai said, is this gunny sack.' (5) Wherever she went, her gunny sack went with her. And after her violent death in Canada, the entire saga of narratives pours out of the mementos preserved in the sack. It is the story of the changing fortunes, across continents, of the villagers of Junapur in India, converted to 'an esoteric sect of Islam that considered thundering Allah as simply a form of reposing Vishnu.' (7) Ji Bai is the narrator-protagonist Salim Juma's chief inspiration, and endearingly he calls her Shehrbanoo—Shehru, for short—thereby making the novel a literary descendent of *The Arabian Nights*. This narrative device also establishes a link between Vassanji and Salman Rushdie, his immediate predecessor in the genre of the Indian immigrant fiction in English. In the manner of *Midnight's Children* of Rushdie, *The Gunny Sack* records the crazy dance of history involving the Cutchi- Gujarati speaking Shamsis. It also explains the logic behind the mad parade of names among the descendants of Dhanji Govindji, who, as a young man aspiring after wealth and success, travels, across the Arabian sea to land at Zanzibar, and from there moves inland to Tanzania. Vassanji writes of him:

> Dhanji Govindji. How much lies buried in a name. . . . Dhan, wealth; Govind, the cowherd butter-thief gopi-seducer, dark Krishna. A name as Banya in its aspiration for wealth as Hindu; yet gloriously, unabashedly, Muslim. For the esoteric sect of the Shamsis there was no difference. (10)

Among other things, Ji Bai's sack contains three pad-locked books in a form of Devnagari, of which the Gujarati script is only one example. This is discovered by Sona, the scholarly brother of Kala, otherwise known as Salim Juma. And, thus, emerges the spicy mass of memory, which, eventually, finds its way into *The Gunny Sack*.

Vassanji's novel includes a large slice of his African experience, which is confined to the East-African coastal regions like Zanzibar, Uganda, Tanzania and Kenya. But at the back of the real-life locations looms the dark and mysterious presence of the vast African continent. This realization dawns on Dhanji Govindji early in his trading career: "Africa was not as small as he had once confidently thought. It was more than the towns and the markets and the caravan routes. One could go deeper and deeper into it and perhaps never return." (32)

In the Dark Continent, the British and the Germans are like two elephants fighting for possessing the land. The native people are like the grass that gets trampled upon, but they are persistent, and keep growing and proliferating. Salim Juma, going to school at Dar-es-Salaam, perceives the subtle changes that come with the gradual awakening of the sleeping continent. He makes note of the fact how Chinua Achebe and Wole Soyinka replace Charles Dickens and John Buchanan in the curriculum. Yet, from a young boy's point of view, Independence, when it finally comes, means only the replacement of the red, white and blue Union Jack by the green, black and gold flag of Tanzania.

The Gunny Sack vividly portrays the transplanted Indian Gujarati identity as it continues to flourish in this alien land. It is present in the game of *antakhshri* that the women play in their rare times of leisure, and it reverberates in the Muslim prayers and the Hindu bhajans of Mad Mitha, the maternal grandfather of Salim Juma. The collective memory of the Gujarati Muslims of Tanzania includes the Hindu concept of *karma* that a soul acquires over many incarnations, involving all kinds of sins and merits. It is not for nothing that Vassanji harps on the responsibility of the daughters-in-law to preserve the *khandaanity* of a family. Ji Bai, the daughter-in-law of Dhanji Govindji, has an onerous task indeed, and the gunny sack of her colourful memories preserves for posterity the record of what she and her descendants go through in Africa after she leaves her paternal home in Gujarat, as a young bride, to follow the footsteps of her husband. Salim Juma's mother, Kulsum, observes the Indian traditions when she gives birth to her first child, a daughter named Begum (nicknamed Victoria for her imperial demeanour). Vassanji writes, "Kulsum had gone without meat for the nine months, and not until every girl in the girls' school had been fed pilau and sweets, not until Kulsum had gone to the mosque, placing coconut and shilling . . . on every step as she descended and came home, did she touch meat." (73)

Kulsum feels constrained to placate the gods and goddesses, orthodox and unorthodox, on Salim Juma's behalf, when he lands himself in a mess. Thus are the Hindu and Muslim traditions harmonized in an alien land. Ji Bai learns her art of healing from her sister-in-law on the eve of Hindu Diwali, and yet the prayers are all *ayats* from the *Quran.* Apart from projecting such remarkable religious tolerance, which does not now prevail in depth in India, Vassanji also advocates inter-racial matrimony. He maintains, "When people of two races combine, beautiful children are born with the virtues of both races." (185)

The Indian connection is again suggested in the detailed nostalgic description of the wedding of a daughter, in which the most memorable part is the farewell and last ceremony. There is also the consciousness of the Indians having barged into Africa with their big black trunks. Salim Juma ruminates during his National Service at Camp Uhuru, "I should have come with a small bag, a rucksack. Instead I came with ladoos, jelebis, chevdo. Toilet paper. A woollen suit." (204)

The Indianness of the central figures in *The Gunny Sack* is reiterated time and again by Vassanji through their reflections, observations and reminiscences. Salim Juma, while doing his stint at the National Service, after the Independence of Tanzania, finds welcome at the Indian mukhi's house in a village. As soon as he enters the house, he notices two giggling young girls. His comment on that episode is revealing: "One takes the sweetness of Indian girls for granted—the playful, even mocking, innocence that evokes tender feelings inside you and you forget how possessive you feel towards them." (208)

Examples like this could be multiplied. One is amused to note how the US Dollar is referred to as 'Ibrahim Bhai' in a currency exchange transaction just because it bears the picture of President Abraham Lincoln. From the USA, a son writes to his mother in Tanzania in Gujarati. The thugs in a godown in Nairobi resemble the Bombay film star, Pran, at his worst. The most significant of all is the advice that Ji Bai's father gives her, after her wedding, at the time of her departure to East Africa. 'Don't let me down Ji Bai. Do nothing to bring shame upon yourself. Never walk out alone. Don't speak of your home outside the four walls. Always cover your family's shame. Don't come back without your husband's permission." (19)

A very important element of the novel is Vassanji's projection of the immigrant experience in East Africa and Canada. The fact of his being part of this scenario lends credibility to his assertions. Nothing could be truer than the statement, 'Governments may come and go, but the immigrants' only concern is the security of their families, their trade and savings.' (52) When Salim Juma thinks back of the school that he attended at Dar-es-Salaam, he is amused to note that his batch included a future motel-chain owner in California, a few smugglers, a thief, two pharmacists, two accountants, a nervous scientist, and a Lisban bar owner. One by one, the young and aspiring boys and girls leave for foreign lands. Someone says on the departure of Yasmin, a cousin of Salim Juma: 'Okay. She's gone. Good bye, Dar, good morning, London. She'll be there in the morning!' (172) That seems to be the fate of most of the younger generation of the Asians in East Africa. The continuous pelting of events batters at the old world, and the broken faith of the immigrants is washed away by the torrents into time's flooding. And, finally, we have the rise to power of Idi Amin in Uganda, and the reign of terror let loose by him on the people of Asian origin, for Allah told him in a dream that they were sabotaging the economy, and not allowing their daughters to marry the Africans. Therefore, Allah concluded, according to the Ugandan dictator, the Asians must go. And they went away from East Africa to England, to the USA, to Canada. That is how the woes of the immigrants spread to the north and the west, and led to the genesis of *The Gunny Sack*, a novel of multiple flavours, a veritable cocktail of a novel. But its chief ingredient is that of the immortal human spirit, which knows no geographical, ethnic or cultural barriers.

M.G. Vassanji's remarkable novel about immigrant experience belongs, perhaps, more with V.S. Naipaul's *A House for Mr. Biswas* and *The Satanic Verses* of Salman Rushdie than with the latter's *Midnight's Children*. Two lessons stand out among several that *The Gunny Sack* presents to the reader. One is that in history and politics there are no heroes. The second is more vital and nearer to truth: 'It is not every day you watch history being made, and know what you're watching is history in the making.' (152)

NOTES

1. Annie Dillard, "Sojourners," *Between Worlds*, ed. Maggie Goh and Craig Stephenson (Oakville, Ontario: Rubicon, 1989), p. 18.
2. Takeo Nakano, "My Hands," frontispiece.
3. Darius Cooper, "What is India to Me . . . I Scream," *The Toronto South Asian Review*, Vol. 10, No. 2, Winter 1992, pp. 47-48.
4. M.G. Vassanji, *The Gunny Sack* (Oxford: Heinemann International, 1989), pp. 248-49.

Immigrant Experience in Canada: M.G. Vassanji's *No New Land*

The novel as a specific literary genre is very much of an English origin, and it developed there in the eighteenth and nineteenth centuries. Since then it has spread, as perhaps the most popular form of literature today, in different countries and continents. But, significantly, the most valuable contributions to this form of writing are now emerging from the erstwhile colonial countries of the former British empire, in other words, from the Commonwealth nations. Raja Rao, Mulk Raj Anand and R.K. Narayan are a trinity of the pioneer Indian writers of English fiction who are still making their valuable contributions to the novel. Rivalling the success of the East-Indian West-Indian brothers, Vidhyadhar Surajprasad Naipaul and Shiva Naipaul, someone who made an impact in the field of Commonwealth fiction was the Nigerian writer, Chinua Achebe. His example inspired another Nigerian, Wole Soyinka, who bagged the 1986 Nobel Award for his contribution to literature—poetry, drama and fiction. Others, whose creative writings have won recognition, are the Kenyan writer, Ngugi wa Thiong'o, and the Nigerian, Ben Okri, author of *The Famished Road*. Most of these writers are active either in their own natural climes or as descendants of their Asian ancestors naturalized in a foreign colonial setting.

During the last two decades of the twentieth century, there has emerged a new set of immigrant writers in the West, in the UK, the USA and Canada, who bring to their works a first hand knowledge of the process of their separation from the lands of their birth, which truly enhances the value of the contribution they are making to the novel. To mention a few among them, I would like to recall the names of the proven literary artists like Salman Rushdie of *Midnight's Children, Shame* and *The Satanic Verses* fame; Bharati Mukherjee with *The Tiger's Daughter, Wife* and *Jasmine*; Rohinton Mistry with *Such a Long Journey* and *Tales from Ferozshah Baug*; Ondaatje, the poet and writer of the Ceylonese origin. The latest in this line is George Seremba, a Ugandan playwright settled in Canada, who wrote a poignant play, *Come Good Rain*, which re-enacts his own attempted execution by the Ugandan forces in a forest outside Kampala. While enacting this play as a solo act, all by himself in a London theatre, he raised his forceful voice against the oppressors of common man like Idi Amin, and in defence of the victims of such oppression. He was invited to present the same play in Kampala itself. In this very context of English writing in the third world, this essay provides a brief analysis of *No New Land*, the second novel of M.G. Vassanji, a Gujarati-Kenyan-Tanzanian Muslim, who lives and writes in Toronto, Canada.

Vassanji is Gujarati and English speaking, and he writes about the frustrating experience of the East-Asian Africans, who were forced to migrate to the USA and Canada following the anti-Asian movement of Idi Amin in Uganda. He was born in Kenya, but got his first education at Dar-es-Salaam in Tanzania. Later, he went to a university in the USA, and finally settled in Canada, where he edits the prestigious *Toronto Review*. Vassanji has an abiding interest in Gujarati and Indian culture. At Haridwar, in March 1994, during a three-day seminar on Canadian literature, organized by the English Department of the Gurukul Kangri University, at which he was a special guest, what impressed me particularly was his absolute secular outlook and interest in the current Indian life and ways of thought. In spite of his African Canadian background, I could appreciate his curiosity about the India of his ancestors. This forms an important aspect of his four works of fiction that have come out so far. *The Gunny Sack* (1989) was a Canadian award-winning first novel that was followed by *No New Land* (1991). These were succeeded by a collection of short stories, *Uhuru Street* (1992) and the latest novel, *The Book of Secrets* (1994).

As in his other three works, in *No New Land* too, Vassanji concentrates on the immigrant experience of some Gujarati-speaking people whose ancestors went away from India to East Africa, and who themselves have been uprooted from there to eventually settle in Canada. The novel is a fictional account of the cycle of migration actually experienced by Vassanji's own family. Nurdin Lalani, his wife Zera, daughter Fatima, and son Hanif, are forced to leave Dar-es-Salaam in the wake of the Idi Amin crackdown on the Ugandans of the Asian origin, which had its repercussions in the neighbouring states of Kenya and Tanzania. The Lalanis are drawn to Toronto by the lure of the safe haven in Canada after they are turned away from London following an immigration check at Heathrow airport. But adjusting to life in the new environment is not so easy as at first they thought it to be. The brunt of this ordeal is borne by Nurdin, the head of the family and the protagonist of *No New Land*. During his first year in Toronto, he applies for scores of jobs, but each time draws a blank. Most advertisers turn him down for his lack of Canadian experience. Having worked for long in the family business of shoes at Dar, he has high hopes of being employed by the proprietor of a footwear department store, but is rejected on the plea of being over-experienced. Vassanji draws the reader's attention to the plight of the Asian immigrants in Canada with a sympathetic sense of irony and almost Dickensian humour. For instance, about the new experience of having to use lifts in the highrise apartment buildings, he has this amusing comment to offer: "it sometimes seems that, against the laws of nature, these elevators go up more times than they go down."[1]

Fatima Lalani, the daughter of the family, has no qualms about the breaking of the bonds of her birthplace in Tanzania. She is ambitious of carving out for herself a rewarding commercial career in Canada, as her ambition is to become rich in the quickest possible time. That, incidentally, happens to be the dream of the majority of the younger generation in India today. Fatima waits expectantly for the letter of admission to a Canadian university that is going to determine the course of her future life. The involvement of her parents in this project is not so deep for they would like to save her from the corrupt influence of the Western culture. The mother's point of view is very significant in projecting the parental attitude: "Their daughter they had perhaps lost already, but she would never lose Hanif. No, not him." (6) The reason behind such thinking is that the people of the Asian origin in Canada do not want to lose their true identity, which is a mixture of Gujarati, Indian and Tanzanian. In the same context, Vassanji makes this significant comment: "We are but creatures of our origins, and however stalwartly we march forward, paving new roads, seeking new worlds, the ghosts from our pasts stand not far behind and are not easily shaken off." (9)

The emotional involvement of the expatriates in Tanzania with their original homeland in India is not to be dismissed off hand. Two elderly men in Dar-es-Salaam, at the Oyster Bay overlooking the Indian Ocean, contemplate "the expanse in front of them and what lay across it: the land of their birth which they had left a long time ago, to which even the longing to return had been muted, although memories still persisted." (10) In Uganda, Gen. Idi Amin overthrew an elected government. He claimed that Allah told him in a dream that the Asians in Africa were exploiters who did not want to integrate with the Africans, and, therefore, they had to go. Perforce, they left Kenya, Uganda and Tanzania, and wound up in Canada and the United States. In Vassanji's novel, Haji Lalani dies believing he has found a new country, Tanzania, for his descendants. But shortly afterwards, his second son, Nurdin, sets off with his own family in search of yet another land. After their rejection by the British, it comes as a pleasant surprise to them when the immigration official at Montreal greets them with a cheering "Welcome to Canada!" (34) The dazzle and sparkle of Toronto is seen as far away as Asia and Africa, where the prospective immigrants dream of foreign goods and the high standard of living. But, on reaching Canada, the initial excitement of the Lalanis is replaced by the disturbing thoughts of reckoning with not too bright a future in an alien land. Soon enough, they realize their position as new Canadians trying to learn from the experiences of the earlier immigrants. After all, Canada is a land chiefly populated by the people of French, English, African, West Indian and Asian origins.

Winter in Canada, especially for the African-Asians, is very harsh and severe for the first time. Surely, there is a big atmospheric difference between 40°C of a Dar summer to 20°C of a Toronto winter. It takes time and patience to get used to the climatic differences. Yet the erstwhile Tanzanians cannot help admiring the first snowfall they witness in Canada: "And when it's snowing there in the night, softly, silently, whitely, you wonder if it's not a childish Christmas card you are dreaming." (59-60)

Vassanji has the knack of bringing us down from the height of fantasy to the depth of reality. This is how he comments on the richness of the immigrant experience in Canada: "the variety found here at Sixty-nine would not be found in any street in Dar. Here a dozen races mingle, conversant in at least as many languages." (60) At the same time, he indicates the exposure to the new world of the young immigrants, who are more impressionable than their seniors: "One envies these children, these darlings of their mothers, objects of immigrant sacrifice and labour who speak better-sounding if not better English: one envies them their memories when they are grown up." (63) In passing, Vassanji also suggests an existential angle in the life of the new Canadian immigrants. Jamal, a lawyer, is discussing with Nanji, a university teacher, the various options open to them in the future. The question boils down to the role of free will in the complicated process of living. In his forthright manner, Jamal demonstrates, "But suppose I use my free will to decide to go on with this absured existence, as they call it," Nanji replies in the fullness of his acquired wisdom, "Well they say that the body has a greater desire to live than the mind to perish." (76) In the same context, Nurdin Lalani compares his lot with that of the younger generation of the immigrants: "What do they know of our weakness, these youngsters, so surefooted in their rarefied world . . . seeing us solid as rocks—and as dumb when all the time there exist thoughts, lurk desires inside you to catch attention and you walk away, heart beating like a shy school girl." (85)

Esmail, a Tanzanian immigrant from Dar, is wantonly bashed up by three white Canadian boys. It becomes a rallying point for the African-Asians in Toronto, and they rush to the succour of their crippled comrade and his wife. Nanji, the thinking immigrant, is understandably depressed after this shocking incident, because he was a helpless spectator to the actual incident. He could himself have been the victim of this senseless racial brutality. "In that very real sense, he too had been attacked." (97) But the new immigrants in Toronto are there to stay and no push-overs. The change in the food habits is another serious problem. The Muslims from Tanzania are not supposed to eat pork. One day, Nurdin, out of curiosity, partakes of a sausage out of the lunch packet of a fellow worker, Romesh by name. Vassanji's comment on this incident expresses the general attitude of the Muslim immigrants in Canada: "Slowly the bestial traits—cruelty and promiscuity, in one word, godlessness—overcame you. And you became, morally, like them. The Canadians." (127) And yet, there are other pulls at heart-strings of an immigrant. He cannot absolutely get away from his emotional involvement with Dar or even remoter India. It is evident in the tempting invitation Nurdin receives from Sushila, the old Tanzanian flame of his elder brother: "Come home" she said finally, "even by losing your way sometime. She used an old turn of phrase." (115)

The sense of exile in Canada persists, even after years of hard intimate living in the new environs. Nurdin cannot forget that he was born in Tanzania, and Canada could never be his real home: "Gone were the days of the fullness of heart, the sense of wholeness at having children. Time was when it was children that brought a man rushing home. . . . But this country had taken his children away, and he felt distanced, rejected by them." (166) However hard they try to make their home in Toronto close to the one left behind in Dar, the outcome is not quite the same. Invariably the spirit and sparkle, that intangible which lights up the atmosphere, is missing. The surprising reappearance in Toronto of the old cap of his father comes as a veritable shock to Nurdin. "He could touch it and in a sense touch his father, smell it and catch a whif of the old man's head, the hair oil used." (196) Yet, Toronto is to his Amarpur, a veritable eternal city, in quest of which his ancestors in India embarked several hundred years ago. But the question remains whether the Asian immigrants from Africa have really reached their destined land.

The conclusion that is forced on the reader, at the end of Vassanji's *No New Land*, is that the search for an ideal home, away from the original home, is the eternal quest of all immigrants, whichever the part of the world they emigrate from and wherever they immigrate to. The dream of pursuing the mirage of a Utopia, whatever the individual compulsions, is universal and never-ending. The grass always appears greener on the other side of the hedge, mountain, border, and even across the seven seas. The actual realization of that dream is a rare fortunate occurrence. Still the dreamers persevere, and the hazy outline of the fruition of the dream looms large in the distant future. This is the predicament of the immigrants all over the world. Had Nurdin Lalani's dream come true, of which there never was any chance, the freedom it would have led him to "now seemed remote and unreal" (208); it had receded into the distance, into another and unknowable world.

NOTE

1. M.G. Vassanji, *No New Land* (Penguin, 1992), p. 2.

The Immigrant Experience of Displacement, Exile and Homelessness in V.S. Naipaul's *A House for Mr. Biswas*

The commonwealth literature of today is a by-product of the ninteenth century British Empire. Whichever part of the world the English eventually withdraw from, they left behind there the legacy of their language and literature. The English works of the creative writers of the erstwhile colonies of the Empire are now vying for honours with the very best that England is producing. The most talked about writer in the English speaking world today is Salman Rushdie, who thrives on the controversial content of his fictional works. But the true successor to the legacy of Charles Dickens, perhaps the greatest English novelist of all times, is V.S. Naipaul, an expatriate from Trinidad, who chose to make England his home. For nearly forty years, he has been entertaining his readers all over the world with a mixed bag of writing that combines fiction with travelogue, journalese and autobiography. Apart from his mastery of the English language, the judicious mix that Naipaul provides is spiced with the flavour of humour, irony and satire that links him with his illustrious predecessor of the Victorian age.

There is, however, one thing that distinguishes Naipaul from Dickens, and that is the background of his colonial antecedents. While it is difficult to dissociate Dickens and his works from London, there is no single city in Trinidad, England, or even India with which you could associate Naipaul. In absolute terms, he belongs to none of these three nations, though all the three contributed to the forming of his sensibility as a writer. The complexity of his multi-faceted yet exclusive personality is a significant contributory factor to the diversity of appeal that one finds in his literary works. The West Indians regard him as an English man because of his British education; the English look upon him as an Indian for his ancestry and the colour of his skin; and the Indians refer to him as a West Indian writer. This is, sometimes, confusing to the research scholars, who would like to approach him as a writer pure and simple. That is how it is in the last decade of the twentieth century, when sociology, history, politics, reality and literature are talked about in the same breath. Much of this controversial debate, today, is due to the question of identity, which crops up again and again in the context of works of literature. It should be a useful exercise to focus attention on the basic problem of the origins of a writer, something that ultimately determines both the complexity and individuality of his work.

The roots of Naipaul's early writings like *The Mystic Masseur* (1957), *The Suffrage of Elvira* (1958) and *Miguel Street* (1959), lie in his Indian background originating in the mixed society of Trinidad. It was a society of the South Asian immigrants, who went to the West Indies in the nineteenth century as indentured labourers to replace the Africans, who became free after the abolition of slavery. Some of these poor labourers, taken away from the remote villages of U.P. and Bihar in India, were put to work in the sugarcane farms of Trinidad. Attracted by the incentives of better wages and avenues in another part of the British Empire, they willingly forsook their homes and hearts, kith and kin, to explore the possibilities of success in an alien land. But the journey across the seas meant a traumatic break from their moorings, traditions and beliefs. On reaching the new country, and after going through the experience of settling in, they invariably tried to revive their links with the land of their origin. Hence, they retained their Hindi speech at home though forced to speak English in the streets, and also continued to follow the Indian social and religious practices in Trinidad or other parts of the West Indies, wherever they were settled. This is evident in the Trinidad works of both V.S. Naipaul and his brother, Shiva Naipaul. The obvious conclusion arrived at even by a casual reader is that these two writers are projecting their sense of displacement, exile and homelessness in their works.

In V.S. Naipaul's *A House for Mr. Biswas* (1961), we encounter three generations of the Indian immigrants in Trinidad, i.e., Bipti and Raghu, Sharma and Mr. Biswas, Anand and his siblings. They correspond to Naipaul's own grandfather, who initially emigrated from India; father, who was born and bred in Trinidad, and worked in the education department there; and Vidyadhar Surajprasad himself, who went to England on a scholarship for university education in 1950, and settled there to become a writer of international reputation. This tells the corresponding story of the other West Indians of Indian origin who live in Trinidad and Guyana, and yet retain links with the motherland of their ancestors. Even now they "come home" when they return to India to visit their relations on places of worship they regard as holy. The trauma as well as joy of such a "return" was experienced by V.S. Naipaul and M.G. Vassanji at different times in their literary careers. It is hard for the expatriates to break their links with India, though most of them no longer speak Hindi or any other Indian language. The predicament of the original immigrants is sensitively expressed by Naipaul in *A House for Mr. Biswas*: "They could not speak English and were not interested in the land where they lived; it was a place where they had come for a short time and stayed longer than they expected. They continually talked of going back to India, but when the opportunity came, many refused, afraid of the unknown, afraid to leave the familiar temporariness. And every evening they came to the arcade of the solid, friendly house, smoked, told stories, and continued to talk of India."[1]

When one is not quite sure of where one belongs, it is of utmost importance to have a roof over one's head. This is a desire of universal nature. Naipaul highlights this basic human yearning by making it the central theme of *A House for Mr. Biswas.* In doing so, he is not only voicing the cherished desire of his protagonist, but of all the other Indian immigrants in Trinidad, who wished for a part of India in the foreign land where they lived. Mr. Biswas's ambition is to possess an exclusive house, a home for himself and his family.

The achievement of this dream would give him a sense of security, warmth and independence, denied to him since his birth in a village in Trinidad. This yearning is symptomatic of his sense of displacement and rootlessness. In spite of the limitations and flaws of the house, he draws satisfaction from the fact that he has paid the cost of the house in full, and that nobody could evict him from his safe haven of peace. To Mr. Biswas, this freedom is a great contrast to living in the houses of the Tulsies, the upper middle class family of his wife: "And now at the end he found himself in his own house, on his own half-lot of land, his own portion of the earth." (8) At the age of forty-six, Mr. Mohan Biswas dies in his own house. During the many years of his active life in different parts of Trinidad, he acquires many things, which he could call truly his own, the fruits of his own labour. "But bigger than them all was the house, his house. How terrible it would have been, at this time, to be without it: to have died among the Tulsies, amid the squalor of that large, disintegrating and indifferent family—to have lived even without laying claim to one's own portion of the earth." (13-14)

The conclusion is obvious. Every individual in the world, however low his social and economic status, desires to possess some space that could be his very own, his house or home. This desire is more evident in people who, for some reason or other are displaced from their origins, and for whom homelessness is an everyday phenomenon. The realization of their rootlessness forces them to create a solid home-space even in an alien land, just as Mr. Biswas does at Port-of-Spain. Through him, Naipaul speaks for the displaced people all over the world.

NOTE

1. V.S. Naipaul, *A House for Mr. Biswas* (Harmondsworth: Penguin, 1969), p. 194.

Sophocles' Oedipus and R.K. Narayan's Raju

In his introduction to modern Commonwealth and South African fiction, entitled *Among Worlds*, William H. New describes the thematic parallels that mark the contemporary literature of each Commonwealth culture. At the same time, he examines some of the ways in which the writers have used their culture's preoccupations to construct separate and multiple worlds. The point that New emphasizes is that "while the separateness reflects their sometimes sharp, sometimes clouded insight into both their own and their society's distinctiveness, the multiplicity demonstrates their unrelenting awareness of the distance between themselves and the traditional ways of life. They are conscious almost always of trying to make sense out of the chaos of the modern world, a chaos which their own local history seems to intensify."[1] What New is stressing here is the unity in diversity of the Commonwealth literature and the writer's attempts to make sense out of the chaotic situation.

My idea of a parallel, however remote, between Sophocles' *Oedipus Rex* and R.K. Narayan's *The Guide* is built round those very assumptions. If it is worthwhile to compare the works of any two individual writers of two separate Commonwealth countries, such as England and India, or the West Indies and India, it is equally worthwhile to compare an ancient Greek tragedy and a modern Indian novel. I do not want to suggest that, at the time of his writing of *The Guide*, Narayan was aware of the connection between the sublime and tragic figure of Oedipus and his own modest unself-confident, Indian middle-class Raju. Though the methods and manner of Sophocles and Narayan are so vastly different, yet a parallel between the two exists, which I have tried to explore. The validity of such a comparison is strengthened further by their attempt to find some sense in the chaos of their own times.

In *Oedipus Rex* and *The Guide*, the basic parallelism is between the central figures of Oedipus and Raju. If Oedipus is the saviour of the Thebans, Raju may be regarded as the pseudo-saviour of the people living in and around the Mangala village. In this connection, it is worthwhile to turn one's attention to the opening of Sophocles' play. As a consequence of Apollo's wrath, drought and pestilence have laid waste the state of Thebes. In the words of the Priest, there is

> Death in the fruitful flowering of her soil
> Death in the pastures: death in the womb of women.[2]

People are suffering, and in desperation they turn to the only saviour that they know of i.e. Oedipus, a stranger among them, who saved them once from the ominous presence of the sphinx, and could perhaps save them again. King Oedipus's reaction to the application of his subjects clearly brings out his nobility:

> I grieve for you my children. Believe me, I know
> All that you desire for me, all that you suffer,
> And while you suffer, none suffers more than I.
> You have your several griefs, each for himself:
> But my heart bears the weight of my own, and yours,
> And all my people's sorrows. I am not asleep.
> I weep: and walk through endless ways of thought. (27)

When we turn from the grim beginning of *Oedipus Rex* to the concluding chapter of *The Guide*, we discover a classic case of unintentional literary parallelism. The destructive ogres of drought and pestilence have once again raised their heads, not in ancient Thebes, but in the remote Indian village of Mangala, accessible to the outside world through the railway station at Malgudi. The crops have failed, the cattle are dying; there is scarcity of water even for domestic purposes; the people are hunted by the fear of the unknown. They keep scanning the sky for any sign of benign clouds, but not a speck is to be seen anywhere. The water-holes are drying up. What is to be done if no rains come? In desperation, the villagers of Mangala turn to the holy man who appears from somewhere, and takes shelter in the old temple near the river bed.

The Greeks of the fifth century B.C. were men of faith. They believed in fate and destiny, in sin and retribution, in Nemesis, in the power of their gods and the vision of their prophets. The stricken Thebans had faith in the Oracle of Delphi, in the prophetic vision of Teiresias, in the capacity of their king to pull them out of their trouble. The present-day Indians, especially the villagers, are not much different in the blind assurance of their own faith. They believe in sadhus and swamis, in the holy men and miracle men, in the efficiency of fasts and penance. Mahatma Gandhi used to undertake fasts for the purification of his soul, and to settle political issues. The villagers of Mangala are simple in their faith. Their drooping spirits get a fillip when Raju threatens to go on fast if they do not stop their quarrels. They have great faith in the powers of the pseudo-holy man Raju, who has recently come to their village, and whom they address as "the Swami." One among them speaks for all:

> This Mangala is a blessed country to have a man like the Swami in our midst. No bad thing will come to us as long as he is with us. He is like Mahatma. When Mahatma Gandhi went without food, how many things happened in India: This is a man like that. If he fasts there will be rain. Out of his love for us he is undertaking it. This will surely bring rain and help us.[3]

The point that needs to be clarified here is that Raju, when he comes to Mangala, or even when he threatens to go on fast, is no holy man. He has been recently released from jail, and is looking for a place where nobody could recognize him, and connect him with his dark past. There is no touch of a saint about him, and he is least interested in masquerading as a miracle man. But the dire need of the villagers, coupled with his own gentleness of heart and flair for helping others out of trouble, thrusts sainthood upon him, which he now finds difficult to get rid of. He saves and hides a few morsels of food, but those do not last him beyond a couple of days. He does not want to be a martyr. Having always been in love with life and its good things, he very much wants to live after turning a new leaf. But the villagers, his ardent admirers, will not let him go. They are determined to kill him with their own brand of kindness. In desperation, Raju as a last resort takes refuge in truth by confessing his tarnished past to Velan, who had discovered him for the villagers. On the other hand, truth is what Oedipus lives and dies for: whatever his faults as a man—*hubris*, irascibility, tyrannous rage—Oedipus is the noble man of truth. Once he initiates the enquiry for locating the killer of Laius, nothing daunts him, nothing stops him, not even the thought of his own destruction. Raju's helplessness is a far cry from the tragic grandeur of Oedipus in his unrelenting pursuit of the search for identity, but he too becomes a man of truth in his own modest way. He too has a problem of identity. Oedipus is sincere and honest but at the same time self-deceived. So long as the First Shepherd insists that it was a band of robbers, and not a single man, that attacked Laius and his party at a place where three roads meet, Oedipus feels assured that he had nothing to do with the murder of Laius. His self-deception also springs from the false belief that he is the son of Polybus, king of Corinth. It is interesting to note in this context what William

Walsh believes to be the central theme of *The Guide*: "The complex association of sincerity and self-deception is indeed the organizing theme of *The Guide*: how these conditions grow out of one another, how they co-exist: disagree, supplant and in the long run re-attract one another."[4] Raju is honest to the extent that he sincerely offers his services as a guide to all newcomers to Malgudi, but he is self-deceived in his prejudiced assessment of Marco and his work, as also in the thinking that Rosie cannot manage without him.

It is Raju's fate to live in public places. Wherever he is, whatever the circumstances, he cannot avoid the limelight. Even in jail he is a model prisoner who catches the eye of the Superintendent. Much earlier, at the station, he comes to be known as Railway Raju, the perfect guide. By becoming a guide, he takes the first step towards his ultimate destiny, which was to be a *guru* (teacher), Swami, and miracle man. In each situation of his life he responds in the way that the people with whom he has dealings want it to be. The same fate overtakes Oedipus, whether overpowered by the Oracle of Delphi or confronted with the misery of his own people. At the end of his chequered career, Raju emerges as a man deserving of the confidence of the simple villagers who have such absolute faith in him: he sacrifices himself to make their dream true. Oedipus never stoops so low as to lose the confidence of his people. In spite of the accusations made by Creon and Teiresias, he retains their faith, and, after his self-banishment, achieves a high spiritual status by his death at Colonus. His act of self-blinding is an act of liberation, and is comparable to Raju's accepting the role of a miracle man when it is thrust on him. As Meenakshi Mukherjee observes, "Towards the end Raju loses the feeling of an actor performing an act: the act becomes the reality, the mask becomes the man, and Raju the guide turns into a Guru."[5]

It is this very play-acting part of Raju's character which, in the final analysis, distinguishes him from Oedipus, who remains always true to himself. In fact, the distinction arises out of the difference of the modes to which *Oedipus Rex* and *The Guide* belong: the former is in the high mimetic mode, while the latter is in the low mimetic mode.[6] Whereas Sophocles employs tragic irony in his presentation of Oedipus, Narayan is being gently satiric in his portrayal of Raju, a modest middle class man. Oedipus is aware of his noble birth and superior intellect, and takes pride—to the extent of *hubris*—in the exercise of his powers. But Raju has the knowledge of his limitations, and works well within them. Yet it is possible to talk of them together, as there are links that unite one tragic figure in literature with another. The separateness of cultures, modes and worlds is no reason for overlooking the unifying fac-

tors which bring one work of art close to another, thereby proving that all writers are basically confronted with the same problems of making sense out of the chaos of existence.

NOTES

1. (Ontario: Porcepic Press, 1975), p. 1.
2. Sophocles, *The Theban Plays* (Harmondsworth: Penguin, 1953), p. 26.
3. R.K. Narayan, *The Guide* (Mysore: Indian Thought Publications, 1966), p. 90.
4. *R.K. Narayan* (London: Heinemann, 1982), p. 114.
5. *The Twice Born Fiction* (New Delhi: Arnold-Heinemann, 1974), p. 124.
6. Northrop Frye, *Anatomy of Criticism* (Princeton: Princeton University Press, 1957), p. 34.

Native and Alien Grounds: Shiv K. Kumar's *Trapfalls in the Sky*

Trapfalls in the Sky, the fifth collection of Shiv K. Kumar's poetry, consists of forty-three enjoyble poems; it is divided into three parts: 'On Native Grounds, 'Under Alien Skies' and 'Genesis.' The first is the largest section with thirty poems, and it provides a panorma of the poet's Indian experiences. The second part has seven poems, written mainly in New York and London. The last section of six poems in inspired by the First Book of the Old Testament.

Some fine poems stand out in this anthology. 'Dal Lake: Srinagar' is a good example of how the atmosphere of a place can inspire a poet to excel himself. Those who know the Dal Lake and its environs re-live the experience of being there when they read the poem. The mood of the beautiful morning born out of the womb of time' is appropriately caught in these lines:

> It's daybreak—the moment of embrace
> between rose and briar, dream and reality,
> faith and negation.

Shiv Kumar's perceptive observation is apparent in 'the sunlight now caresses the camel-caravan of hilltops, their necks drooping'; the aptness of comparison is visually striking in 'the chinars, stately like turbaned watchmen'; 'A spectral skiff propelled by lunar force' provides a Coleridgean echo. The waters of the lake become audible in their 'lisp and gurgle and kiss,' as the boat glides over its smooth surface. The 'primeval crystal' of the first line, linked with the 'conjuror's crystal' of the last line, indicates the perfect circular structure of the poem.

'Cleansing Ganga' is obviously suggested by the anti-Ganga-pollution campaign. The images of the downy chick, littlum calf and undiapered babe—all creatures 'chaste like breast-milk' at nativity—hint at the purity of the river at its source. The cunning and corrupt priests confront the reader in

> The noontime sweat oozing from the saffron
> stripped foreheads of the crocodiles.
> Whose yawning jaws chant mantras in
> some obsolete tongue.

The contrast of the two sets of images imaginatively sums up the problem of the Ganga's pollution.

The very first poem in the collection, 'Mother Teresa Feeds her Lepers at her Home for the Destitute, Calcutta,' celebrates the great humanitarian work that 'the Virgin's brides-maid' from Yugoslavia has been doing in India for about half a century. 'She is a shaft of sun-beam . . . beckoning the dead to rise,' and is contrasted with Kali the 'Goddess in stone,' with her 'face ebony, eyes the colour of blood.' The earthly compassion of a living saint raises her above the savage tantric stance of a primitive goodness. Similarly, the poem entitled 'The Holocaust Survivor' commemorates the experience of Arnost Lustig, the Czechoslovakian novelist, who survived the Nazi concentration camp at Auschwitz:

> All that happened long ago
> before the first man swallowed
> his primal shame.

Here the birth of human suffering is connected by the poet with the Original Sin. He also suggests a possible solution to it through the defiant spiritual strength of Man:

> The only way to vanquish the sun
> is to glower back
> into his vitals.

Shiv Kumar's keen sense of irony is noticed in 'My Adolescent Son's Room,' where

> Some books
> untouched like nuns
> perch demurely
> waiting for even a side-glace.

His power of ironic observation is again evident in 'A Young Female Jogger':

I've conspired with the trees
and lamp-posts along your track
to turn on their camera's fast shutters
as you zip through the stratosphere.

The dominant metaphoric theme of *Trapfalls in the Sky* moves through its pages like a structural refrain. It is sexual symbolism and the imagery of love that link together most of these poems into a series of passionate encounters. 'An Indian Mother's Advice to her Daughter before Marriage' begins with these lines:

giving up all your hoardings
before dying
may not be entirely painful
for the first bleeding that splutters
like oil on fire is also a cleanser.

Here the act of sexual consummation and loss of virginity takes the form of a ritualistic initiation. The prostitute in 'At a Whorehouse' is asked:

Can you rock me into forgetting
a woman who once promised me
manna in the tulip of her mouth?

The mere act of physical gratification can hardly match the blissful experience that mutual love between man and woman affords. Lust can never rise to the ecstatic heights of love.

There is bold irony in 'A Wayside Shiva Temple':

A Wayside, Lingam-shaped boulder,
behind which I once kneaded a woman's
body,
cannot look me straight in the eye.

Freudian imagery is apparent in the bride's figure in 'Cleansing Ganga':

As she walks into the nuptial chamber
holding a lone candle
to be snuffed out
into the Bay's eternity.

The indiscriminate couplings at the 'Shakespeare Seminar' at Oklahoma University, USA, reduce it to a 'goatish week-end.' There is oriental eroticism in 'Birth of Eve':

> A bosom with two moons
> shoulders like mute doves
> lips like two petals peeled off a gold cup, . . .
> and in her gait the swing of a dancing peacock.

In 'Adam to Eve,' the act of love becomes an act of knowing and dying:

> and if to know is to die
> why not perish together?

Eve reciprocates Adam's feelings by asking

> What turbulence is this
> after a season of placid submission? . . .
> what beast is now crying out within me for redemption?

Trapfalls in the Sky provides many echoes of classical Indian writers like Kalidasa and Vatsyayana. That is understandable, and also as it should be. But the less frequent and persistent touches of Yeats and Eliot appear rather out of place. 'Baptism of Fire' is a poem of adolescent love, encroached upon by the sacred thread ceremony. The sacrificial fire reminds the young novice of the fire of passion lit by the touch of his girl's

> nascent breasts under the mango tree, . . .
> and the earth spins on a bull's horns
> for a new gyre.

So obvious a Yeatsian image fails to satisfy the discerning reader all set to enjoy the Indianness of experience in Shiv Kumar's poetry. The parody of Eliot's *The Waste Land* that follows in the same poem, does not enhance one's pleasure in this bunch of otherwise perceptive and skilfully composed poems. A similar feeling of unacceptance is aroused by 'High Fever,' where the persona feels, 'trapped in a paradox,' and his

> eye-balls sizzle like egg-yolk
> in a frying pan.

But 'O Delhi' pulls one back from the artificiality of Western sensibility to authentic Indian realism. The 'caravan of exiles,' following the partition, leads to the 'gray shawl of mist' and 'the gazals of Ghalib and Zauq.' The young city whose

> streets and alleyways were like the contours
> of a virgin's torso-taut and scented,

is now grown into 'an old matron with sagging udders and plastic dentures.' Time takes its toll of all things—of cities, of passion, of men and women!

Hymn to Humanity: Kulothungan's *Earth is Paradise Enough*

On picking up this slim volume of poetry, one is intrigued by the name of the author. It is the pen-name under which Professor V.C. Kulandai Swami, the eminent hydrologic engineering expert and the former Vice-Chancellor of Indira Gandhi National Open University, New Delhi, writes his Tamil poetry. Kulothungan I (1070-1120 AD) was a Chola King, who maintained the integrity of his Andhra territories for half a century. According to K.M. Panikkar, the historian, he was "one of the greatest of the Chola monarchs [who] added the victories of peace to the victories of war."

The forty-eight poems included in *Earth is Paradise Enough* are selected and translated by the author himself from three out of four volumes of Tamil poems, published during the last forty years. Two poems, 'My Writer Friend' and 'Jewels Turn into Leeches,' are translated by Prema Nandakumar. The three volumes of Tamil poetry, from which the poems in the present volume are drawn, are *Vaayil Thirakkattum* (Let the Gates Open), *Vinn Samaippov Varuha* (Welcome to Those Who Could Create a Heaven) and *Kathavuhal Kaappathillai* (No Fortress for Protection). U.R. Anantha Murthy, President, Sahitya Akademi (that honoured the poet with an award in 1988), writes about him in the Foreword, "His poetry is eminently that of a citizen whose creative imagination works for a stable and integrated civilization. It does not have the arrogance of a technocrat who wants to conquer nature." This well-considered judgment of the author of *Samskara* sums up the general tone of and the world-view expressed in the poems, which justify the poet's choice of 'Kulothungan' as his pen-name.

From his very childhood, the poet—as he writes in the Preface to *Earth is Paradise Enough*— developed a deep interest in the problems of social reform and social justice. The raw deal meted out to the poor and the downtrodden in our society always filled him with indignation and sorrow, yet his hope for the better times to come remained undiminished. This aspect of Kulothungan's state of mind comes out clearly in poems like 'Even Poverty is Sweet,' 'This is the Law My Child' and

'How Long.' The poet is constrained to admit

> You shall grow and discover
> indignities in exalted positions.
> So ordered is our society, my child!

But he protests,

> Overflowing affluence on one side;
> piercing poverty and pain on the other. . . .
> How long can this the world endure?

The conviction that things shall not remain as they are, but improve with the changing circumstances, is clearly suggested by the questioning in the last line quoted above.

In the very opening poem of the volume, the poet prays for

> A dignified life, noble and cultured
> with the majesty, of a tusker walking
> or a mountain in motion. . . .
> The capacity to create all that we long for,
> The strength to design destiny itself.

His fierce optimism is much in evidence in 'Let's Forge a New World':

> "a sorrowless and painless life
> is realizable here and now. . . "
> Welcome to those who could create a Heaven!

And, again, in these lines:

> Everest is not the only peak,
> Every hillock has a summit to boast!

Kulothungan celebrates 'the muscle and might of performing shoulders,' and salutes 'the feet that tirelessly ascend.'

In the race for achieving higher goals in the world, where 'to be born, to grow, to procreate, to wither with age/and die, is common to every life,' there is little scope for slackening one's steps. The poet reminds man in forceful terms:

> You are the creator of all angels, gods and other

heavenly beings that the world talks about;
You are also the father of the sciences
that destroyed many myths.

Poetry is not a mere reflection of society, but it must lead to action, and provide a vision of the future that man wants to create. But most scriptures assert that God created the universe and everything in it. In this very context, Kulothungan challenges all books of religion with an astounding declaration:

If there be God, I have but
one boon to ask;
"I shall be God myself."

To him, a greater wonder than all the heavenly bodies is the mind of man.' Man combines 'the quiet calm/of a dew drop on a flower' and 'the melting heat of the sun.' There is logic behind his conclusion in 'The Dawn of an Era':

That, which does not change,
does not evolve;
That, which does not evolve,
does not survive.

'Tears' is a moving poem that combines cleansing compassion with a powerful sense of achievement. Tears 'dissolve the harvest stone and melt the/strongest steel.' The poet admires the fortitude of the poor vendor, who spreads his wares under a tree, and he declares,

What if he is poor? In his dignified state
even poverty is sweet.

Kulothungan has a strong sense that the Indians have dismally lagged behind in the race for scientific achievement:

We halted for a second and were
left behind a thousand miles.

But there is hope that, with determination and united effort, we can still make up the lost ground:

For the mind engrossed in the task undertaken

Earth itself is Paradise enough.

Above all, the poet sings in praise of the emergence of knowledge as a major resource of progress and all round development in the world. He regards the scientific temper of man as the major contribution of modern knowledge and learning. It is in this light that he refers to the advance of science and technology in the west.

Kulothungan writes Tamil poetry, not in free verse, but in its classical form. In this volume, it is transliterated into English, and, naturally, shows some drawbacks of being rendered into an alien medium. In its originality, it differs noticeably from the traditional English poetry, even from Indian English poetry, in form and content. At places, the English structures leave scope for improvement, still, *Earth is Paradise Enough* is genuine poetry that does not fail to move the reader. This is particularly true of poems like 'She Keeps Chiselling Me,' 'The Singer and the Song,' and 'Full Moon is No Daily Phenomenon.' It is pieces like these that vindicate the poet's description of the volume as a 'Hymn to Humanity':

The tears that swell and flow down my eyes
serve to cleanse my entire self:
I have come out after a bath in fire.
Shall the heat of a hot day hurt me ever?
She keeps chiselling me further and further.

Index